EXPORTING
AMERICA

EXPORTING AMERICA

*Why
Corporate Greed
Is Shipping
American Jobs
Overseas*

LOU DOBBS

Published by Warner Books

NEW YORK   BOSTON

Warner Business Books
Warner Books

Time Warner Book Group
1271 Avenue of the Americas, New York, NY 10020
Visit our Web site at www.twbookmark.com.

The Warner Business Books logo is a trademark of Warner Books.

Printed in the United States of America

First Printing: August 2004
10 9 8 7 6 5 4 3 2 1

Library of Congress Control Number: 2004106440
ISBN: 0-446-57744-8

To my wife, Debi,
and children, Chance, Jason, Heather, and Hillary

Acknowledgments

First always, thanks to my family for their love and patience.

In taking on the issue of the exporting of American jobs, the staff of *Lou Dobbs Tonight* has been extraordinary in their tireless work to report the facts on outsourcing and offshoring, even when they didn't know where those facts would lead us. My thanks to Bill Dorman, Kevin Burke, Amy Shniderman, Jim McGinnis, Leslie Bella-Henry, Deborah Davis, Peter Viles, Kitty Pilgrim, Casey Wian, Lisa Sylvester, Bill Tucker, Christine Romans, Louise Schiavone, Lisa Slow, Claudine Hutton, Philippa Holland, Mara Wilcox, Adrienne Klein, Rene Brinkley, Nickie Bonner, Charles Hurley, Tom Evans, Marci Starzec, Lisa Martin, Dierdre Hughes, Lisa DiLallo, Jill Billante, and Norm Wong. All of us are fortunate to be a part of CNN and Time Warner, which are committed to world-class journalism. My thanks to Jim Walton for his support and encouragement throughout, to Ken Jautz, Phil Kent, Jeff Bewkes, and our CEO, Dick Parsons. One of the first companies we put on our public list of outsourcing corporations was the AOL subsidiary of Time Warner. Not one executive in any quarter of the company complained. In fact, Dick had the good grace to argue the issue on the program.

My thanks as well to Warner Books boss Larry Kirshbaum, who believed the issue of outsourcing American jobs was so important that it deserved to be a book, Harvey Newquist for constant help and humor in making it so, Christine Brandenburg for always terrific research, and to Slade Sohmer. Thanks to my great agent and friend Wayne Kabak and to my editor, Colin Fox, for applying his wonderful talent with such skill and forbearance.

Contents

EXPORTING AMERICA

For globalization to work for America, it must work for working people. We should measure the success of our economy by the breadth of our middle class, and the scope of opportunity offered to the poorest child to climb into that middle class.

—JOHN J. SWEENEY

We frequently see the respectful attentions of the world more strongly directed towards the rich and the great, than towards the wise and the virtuous. We see frequently the vices and the follies of the powerful much less despised than the poverty and weakness of the innocent.

—ADAM SMITH

Introduction

The power of big business over our national life has never been greater. Never have there been fewer business leaders willing to commit to the national interest over selfish interest, to the good of the country over that of the companies they lead. And the indifference of those business leaders to our long-term national welfare is nowhere more evident than in the exporting of American jobs to cheap overseas labor markets.

The rising debate over the outsourcing of hundreds of thousands of American jobs has revealed a fundamental imbalance in our economy and society. The debate has exposed an altogether too comfortable alliance between multinational corporations and government, which has resulted in Corporate America's dominance over Washington. It has focused our attention on U.S. trade policies that haven't worked for three decades. And, most important, it has raised the question of whether we'll continue to sacrifice our jobs, our middle class, and our national wealth to Corporate America's pursuit of international trade agreements that are "free trade" in name only.

The resolution of the issue will ultimately determine whether our middle class will continue to diminish or will once again flourish; whether we're willing to accept a country that works only for the wealthy and powerful, or will insist on forging a future in which America works for all of us. And at this moment, the outcome is far from assured. Once you've heard what I have to say, I hope you'll agree that outsourcing and the motives behind it are simply destructive of our way of life. And that it has to end.

I've been accused of being too passionate in my criticism of this relatively recent but rapidly growing corporate practice of shipping American jobs to cheap foreign labor markets. Accused of being too concerned about working men and women in this country. Of not understanding that the United States must be ferociously competitive in our globalized economy. A few corporate CEOs have called me a communist, and some Republicans in Congress have called me a protectionist. For the record, I'm neither a communist nor a protectionist. However, some members of the Bush administration consider me to be nothing less than a traitor to their cause of free trade at seemingly any cost to workers and our economy. And more than a few columnists and pundits have charged me with being a raving populist. I'm not always sure which of those slurs is intended to be the worst, but I assure you, the accumulated insults can ruin part of your day—and can sometimes be more than a little bit intimidating.

Of course, intimidation is precisely the desired effect of those insults, slurs, and, in some cases, outright personal attacks. But as often happens in life, unintended consequences have a way of prevailing. That's precisely what happened last year when I decided not just to do an occasional story but instead to commit to constant, almost nightly coverage of the outsourcing of American jobs overseas, on my nightly show on CNN.

That's because instead of being intimidated, my colleagues on the broadcast were struck by the violent reaction to our coverage of the outsourcing issue. Although initially hesitant about the amount of time we were devoting to outsourcing and its effect, our executive producer, Bill Dorman, was among the first to question why so many critics in business, government, and the media were attacking me personally instead of trying to refute my arguments with facts and reason. Our producers, Kevin Burke, Amy Shniderman, Jim McGinnis, and Leslie Bella-Henry, were equally supportive. With Dorman's guidance, correspondents Peter Viles, Kitty Pilgrim, Bill Tucker, Lisa Sylvester, and Casey Wian reported the issue with intelligence and energy, turning up story after story of hardworking Americans who were losing their jobs to foreign workers for no other reason than that they were making a decent living and couldn't compete with someone in China, India, or Eastern Europe who earned a fraction of their wages.

And our viewers, from the first story we reported, have written to us and called us to share their stories of companies laying them off and shipping their jobs to cheap-labor countries such as India. We've heard from literally tens of thousands of people who've lost their jobs, or who have a friend or family member who's lost a job, to outsourcing. And on too many occasions, their companies not only laid them off but then forced them to train their replacements. I still can't understand how anyone could treat a person, a coworker and colleague—a fellow American—like that. Of course, there's a lot about outsourcing that requires some work to understand. Even after researching and reporting the issue from every conceivable angle, I still find it difficult to accept that so many leaders of Corporate America could descend to such a level that they would ship American jobs overseas to achieve what are at best relatively insignificant cost reductions while ignoring the pain of their employees and their families, and the burdens that outsourcing imposes on the communities in which their corporations do business.

I hope you know that I'm no wide-eyed Pollyanna, nor am I a fire-breathing liberal. In fact, I'm a lifelong Republican. I believe deeply in our free-enterprise democracy. I'm a capitalist. I believe in the strength and resilience of this great economy of ours. I've been not only a journalist for three decades but also an executive, a businessman, and an investor. I understand business cycles and the harsh necessity of cutting expenses and laying off employees in down cycles and recessions. But I also know the importance of people, of employees and the need to invest in them. I know the importance of taking a longer view of business cycles, and a broader view of the responsibility owed by business and business leaders, not only to their investors but to *all* the stakeholders in the corporation, including employees, the community, and our country. I strongly believe that corporations should be good citizens.

I also confess to being something of an idealist. While this country is far from perfect, we Americans enjoy a way of life unparalleled in history. Like most Americans, I'm a beneficiary of that way of life and have a deep sense of indebtedness to all who've made my good fortune possible. I was born into a working-class family but never felt truly poor, because I had love and support at home and went to public schools where teachers took the time and interest to nurture all students, no matter their families' wealth or lack of it. And I was taught to respect anyone who worked for a living, no matter what the job or how much it paid. And to appreciate having a job. And my wife and I have tried to pass that along to our children.

I know firsthand the importance of a strong public education and a job in achieving the American Dream, in ensuring for all Americans the opportunity to build a better life than that of their parents. And I cringe when I hear a CEO, a lobbyist, or a politician say they support outsourcing jobs overseas because Americans aren't well enough educated or sufficiently productive. I don't believe it's true. Perhaps some of them sincerely believe what they're saying. But even so, why don't they feel a sense of responsibility to keep workers here employed, to allow their taxes to finance better schools, to invest in the people who will build our future? I think too many people in Corporate America and Washington have forgotten about the dream that should be the birthright of everyone in this country. I hope that after reading this book you'll take time to remind them of the dream. And help keep it alive.

ONE

Assault on Middle-Class Americans

The twentieth century has been characterized by three developments of great political importance: the growth of democracy, the growth of corporate power, and the growth of corporate propaganda as a means of protecting corporate power against democracy.

—ALEX CAREY

The odds are that during the past recession, you or someone you know was affected by corporate layoffs and the loss of a job. It's a painful experience, and one that can have a devastating effect on individuals and families. But in some cases, layoffs have affected entire towns, in effect crippling communities. And layoffs related to outsourcing have long-term effects on those communities, because companies pulling out take their taxes with them—that is, if they paid them at all. And the people in the town are also unable to pay taxes, because they're no longer getting paid to work.

These corporate pullouts run the gamut from manufacturing to high tech. The examples in the next few pages are just a few of the scenarios that are playing out with alarming regularity in communities all across America.

In Syracuse, New York, Carrier, the maker of air-conditioning and heating units, is closing two of its most productive and profitable factories and laying off 1,200 workers. Most of those jobs are headed to Singapore and Malaysia. It's too early for many of Carrier's employees to retire—the average worker at the plant is only forty-nine years old. In a move to save the jobs, New York State and the plant's union tried to dissuade Carrier from exporting the jobs to Asia by offering a $42 million incentive package. To no avail—the company is outsourcing these jobs.

With the closing of the Carrier plant, central New York State has now lost 10,000 jobs since 1990. Senator Hillary Clinton told me that she believes "Manufacturing is not a luxury. It's not an old-fashioned economic activity. It truly is core to much of what we need to do to maintain a strong economy and, I would argue, a strong national defense." Senator Clinton's assessment is close to that of Republican congressman Duncan Hunter, chairman of the House Armed Services Committee. A conservative Republican and a liberal Democrat in agreement on economic issues is a sign that the times, and Washington's policies, could be changing.

Syracuse may be better off than some cities in that it has an anchor industry: higher education. It's home to Syracuse University, and the city has worked hard to diversify its economy in the wake of plant closings by General Motors, General Electric, and Allied Signal. However, even with the anchor of Syracuse University, wage growth in the city has fallen below the national average as manufacturing jobs have left.

What's happening in Syracuse is no different from what is happening in many communities across America. From steel to appliances to automobiles, paying manufacturing jobs are being exported out of the country, leaving behind workers and communities struggling with how to recover.

The automobile industry is a prime example of a business in which ruthless pressure to cut costs has driven jobs abroad. And it affects jobs in many states. At Tower Automotive in Milwaukee, 500 employees used to make the frames for Dodge Ram pickup trucks. Now that work, and their jobs, are going to Mexico. The decision was made by DaimlerChrysler, which is squeezing its American suppliers by asking them to match the lower prices available from overseas manufacturers. All the automakers, not just Chrysler, claim they need these lower prices in order to keep making affordable cars and to keep market share.

Early this year, Ford closed its plant in Edison, New

Jersey, after more than fifty-five years of producing cars and trucks there. A Ford spokesman said it would be too expensive to retool that plant so that it could produce different models. About 300 of the plant's 900 workers were relegated to early retirement, while others were transferred to Ford plants elsewhere in the country. Most important, at least 400 jobs were eliminated. Ford is, however, investing heavily in Asia and has set up a new regional headquarters in Thailand.

General Motors, long the symbol of Detroit's automotive might, has introduced a new Chevy, the Equinox. The Equinox is assembled in Canada with a Chinese-made engine. Now, the three most expensive parts of any automobile are the body, engine, and transmission. With the Equinox featuring a foreign-built engine, more than a third of the vehicle's cost is being transferred—and paid out—to China and not to American suppliers or workers. An interesting statistic: Employment in the U.S. auto industry has dropped by 200,000 jobs over the past four years. During that same time, imports of Chinese auto parts have doubled.

What makes all these examples so frustrating for American workers is that while Detroit throttles back at home and invests in Asia, foreign automakers, including Honda, Nissan, and Toyota, are investing in this market. In fact, as American automakers cut back, these Japanese companies are providing all the production growth in the United States. And calling our American automakers the Big Three is now a myth. Only two companies, Ford and GM, are American-based, while Chrysler is owned by German manufacturer DaimlerChrysler. To put a fine point on it, Toyota is selling more cars in the United States than Chrysler. And Toyota is now the second leading global car company, after General Motors.

We're not faring well in the auto business, and we're not faring well in the appliance business. Galesburg, Illinois, is the birthplace of poet Carl Sandburg and for many years was home to a large Maytag factory. In fact, Galesburg was a Maytag company town, and Maytag provided 1,600 jobs to local workers.

But Maytag decided to close its Galesburg factory and move much of the work to a new refrigerator manufacturing plant in Reynosa, Mexico. None of the American jobs are slated to be transferred—all 1,600 are scheduled to be laid off. Employees who made $15 an hour are being replaced by Mexican workers who earn less than $1 an hour. Maytag justifies the closing by citing competition from cheaper Asian refrigerators, and the tighter wallets of cost-conscious consumers.

With a current jobless rate of 9 percent, Galesburg will soon face a possible unemployment rate of 20 percent, along with a very uncertain future. People there can't turn to the government for help. After all, free trade agreements signed by the government promised workers at plants like this one a chance to export their products to new markets around the world. But the reality is, the only thing being exported from Galesburg is American jobs.

Clintwood, Virginia, has a population of 1,800. It's not a big town, but 250 of its best jobs are in the process of being outsourced to India. Online travel service Travelocity is shutting down its call center here. Workers at Travelocity made a starting wage of $8 an hour, plus training and benefits. But Travelocity lost $55 million last year and was looking to cut costs fast. It decided it could save $10 million by moving its Clintwood call center to India. Travelocity told CNN that "We made a difficult decision to outsource following significant losses last year. Our costs were significantly higher than our major competitors, who had chosen long ago to outsource to the Philippines, India, and elsewhere."

Travelocity is trying to give workers a soft landing by providing eleven months' notice, along with possible interviews at Travelocity's two remaining U.S. call centers. Clintwood, meanwhile, is going back to its roots, marketing one of the few things that can't be outsourced: tourism. Combined with local crafts and a mountain music museum dedicated to a local artist, Grammy Award winner Ralph Stanley, the town is attracting attention to itself. As a final note, the whole Travelocity episode was the second of two body blows to Clintwood. Just before Travelocity set up shop there, Nexus Communications had shut down a similar call center operation in the town.

The people of Celina, Tennessee, have experienced firsthand the cost of free trade. Twelve hundred people once worked in the town's OshKosh plant in Celina. Now only fifteen do. The rest of those jobs were sent out of the country, to Mexico and Honduras. Some of the company's employees had worked at OshKosh for three decades. But with OshKosh gone, the unemployment rate in Celina is 15.5 percent, and its per capita income has fallen to $13,000.

While Celina is just one more town abandoned by American companies in search of cheap foreign labor, the town is fighting to get back on its feet and stay there. Clay County has created a Web site to attract new business to Celina and the surrounding area, and the chamber of commerce is aggressively selling the county to outsiders. It has already been successful, having lured a commonly outsourced business to the town: a call center. Healthcare Management Resources has set up a new center to handle billing for hospitals and now employs 120 people. The jobs don't pay as much as the factory jobs at OshKosh, but it's steady work and it carries benefits. Moreover, the company is thrilled with Celina. According to Dennis

Swartz, the president of Healthcare Management Resources, the people of Celina have a "great work ethic. I put these people up against anybody anywhere. And my goal in life is really to set up a third center, a fourth center, a fifth center in areas just like this."

Internet provider Earthlink is closing its call center in Harrisburg, Pennsylvania, and sending 400 jobs to the Philippines and India. The state of Pennsylvania has already been hard hit by job losses, having seen 132,000 manufacturing jobs evaporate. Now it's seeing its high-tech jobs go away. At a stop in Harrisburg in 2004, President Bush told Pennsylvanians that "There are people looking for work because jobs have gone overseas. And we need to act in this country. We need to act to make sure there are more jobs at home." So far, that has been nothing but an empty statement. And to worsen the pain, the Earthlink workers in Harrisburg have been denied special trade assistance by the Bush administration.

Outside of the obvious factory closings and new call centers in India, there are the insidious under-the-radar cases of outsourcing that we rarely ever detect. They eat away at our economic infrastructure like rot in a foundation, and we barely notice—until it's too late. For example, The Smithsonian Institution has chosen Innodata Isogen to create an online library of one of the most expansive research projects in American history, the United States Exploring Expedition. Running from 1838 to 1842, it was the first federally funded mission of exploration in U.S. history and yielded nearly 3,000 pages of data on topics including geology, anthropology, American art, and more. But Innodata Isogen outsourced the work to the Philippines. According to the Smithsonian, the work was sent overseas because there are not enough skilled workers in this country to do the job. I find it incredibly hard to believe that it required offshore talent to chronicle the legacy of one of America's greatest research endeavors.

Under-the-radar outsourcing affects small industries that have been the source of jobs in the United States for as long as most people can remember. The embroidery industry, one of the mainstays of the New Jersey economy for more than a century, is now in danger of disappearing from this country. Small New Jersey factories once made 90 percent of the embroidery in American lingerie, clothing, and bedding. It was a half-billion-dollar-a-year industry with nearly 7,000 jobs. Today, there are less than 1,000 jobs left. American clothing manufacturers still require embroidery on their products, but they've gone to Sri Lanka, India, China, and Mexico to get it done.

It's doubtful that anyone will claim that embroidery is a critical component of our national economy, yet it is a traditional craft that has provided a good income to thousands of Americans for generations. And there's still a lot of it being done—just not by Americans. It's one more part of apparel manufacturing that is being outsourced. Today, 96 percent of clothing production is done outside our borders. That fact had a direct bearing on last year's closing of thirty-seven textile factories in North and South Carolina alone.

And when it comes to apparel, even gaping loopholes in U.S. Customs inspections of clothing and textiles are costing American jobs. Less than one-tenth of one percent of the three million textile shipments that come into this country every year are inspected. That's a security gap that foreign textile manufacturers have been exploiting to their benefit and our detriment. Knowing that they are unlikely to get caught, unscrupulous producers will label a piece of clothing to read that it was made in, say, Honduras, when it may actually have come from China. Then it's shipped to the United States using falsified entry documents. According to a recent General Accounting Office report, the lack of inspection at our borders results in the frequent smuggling of garments past U.S. customs.

There's even more opportunity for abuse. U.S. Customs allows shippers to pass cargo through the United States, free of charge and free from quota restrictions, on its way to another country. But Customs does not track shipments adequately enough to ensure that they leave the United States. Many shipments get here, claim to be passing through, and are then diverted to store shelves in American cities and towns—without a penny in tariffs ever being paid. This kind of cheating makes it hard for American textile manufacturers to compete. It's not known how much is lost in tariff revenue from this kind of fraud and smuggling, but one case provides some stunning insight. In Long Beach, California, 5,000 containers were stopped and inspected. Customs agents found illegal merchandise. The exporter was trying to avoid paying $65 million in duties.

The final indignity is that these imports, both legal and illegal, are usually arriving on foreign-owned ships. Seven hundred fifty billion dollars' worth of goods comes into the United States on ships each year, but not one of the top ten international shipping companies is American-owned. Foreign companies have bought out nearly all the top American cargo carriers—a trend that has been facilitated by foreign governments that subsidize their international shipping companies. American firms sold out when they realized they couldn't compete against subsidized international shipping. Free trade or simply the absence of an American trade strategy?

These foreign ships are arriving in American port terminals that are increasingly under the control of foreign companies. An estimated 50 percent of East Coast terminals and 30 percent of West Coast terminals are leased and operated by foreign companies—not by U.S. businesses.

If you look at every one of these companies, industries, towns, and communities, outsourcing has far-reaching and devastating effects across all aspects of our society. Yet there is still one more insidious element: the growing multibillion-dollar industry made up of companies that are actually getting paid to help other companies outsource their businesses. Many of the companies exporting American jobs to cheap foreign labor markets are not doing it by themselves, and there are a lot of consultants anxious to help.

U.S. businesses spent $16 billion on outsourcing work last year, according to leading IT research company Gartner Inc. But outsourcing overseas often means that corporations have to rely on consulting firms that specialize in outsourcing. Consultants often play a role as the middleman, connecting companies with offshore providers and holding conferences to help companies outsource and "offshore" work. This past year, at a New York City hotel, corporate executives paid $500 apiece for advice on how to export American jobs to cheap overseas labor markets. Protesters got wind of the conference and picketed with signs reading, "Be American. Buy American."

But inside the hotel, the signs celebrated offshore outsourcing. Consulting firm Covance bragged that "We pioneered the transparent offshore outsourcing model." Executives attending the event learned the finer points of doing business in emerging labor markets such as Russia, the Philippines, and Vietnam. The cosponsor of the event, Atul Vashistha, CEO of NeoIT, told our reporter Peter Viles that "in the short term, this is a painful process. No question about it. But in the medium to long term, you will create more jobs on the services side of the economy." When Viles asked him where all those new jobs would be, Vashistha cited global business management, which, among other things, is managing all the jobs that companies outsource.

One seminar was intriguingly titled, "Is Offshore Sourcing Unpatriotic?" Even more intriguing, that seminar was closed to the news media, so we never did get the answer to the question posed by the seminar. But I'm sure I could have guessed what the sponsors would have said.

The thing that's not being communicated at these conferences is that American multinational companies that are outsourcing and offshoring are also essentially firing their customers. India can provide our software; China can provide our toys; Sri Lanka can make our clothes; Japan can make our cars. But at some point we have to ask, what will *we* export? At what will Americans work? And for what kind of wages? No one I've asked in government, business, or academia has been able to answer those questions.

——

TWO

What Right to Work?

I believe in the dignity of labor, whether with head or hand, that the world owes no man a living, but that it owes every man an opportunity to make a living.

—JOHN D. ROCKEFELLER

Hewlett-Packard chairwoman and CEO Carly Fiorina recently declared that "No American has a God-given right to a job." My first reaction when I read her statement was, "Go to hell, Carly." That first reaction has held up as a lasting impression. As much as I hate what she said, I at least have to give Fiorina credit for straight talk. She didn't sugarcoat her sentiments for public consumption, because she didn't have to. Forty or fifty years ago, Fiorina's bald statement, and its clear implications, would have fueled a firestorm of labor protest and political controversy. Not now. Working men and women in this country aren't part of the political equation. Business and capital rule. It's that simple.

How has Corporate America reached such a pinnacle of power that there is seemingly no countervailing influence to its primacy over public policy and international trade? The answers are complex and varied. Globalization and technology have transformed our industrial economy into one of services and knowledge-based enterprises. Our population has doubled in the past forty years, and while we can proudly boast of being the most diverse society in the world, identity politics have superseded grassroots participatory pluralism. We have become a nation where affiliation with a political party and its ideology has become more important—and easier—than dealing intelligently with specific issues on a case-by-case basis. The result is that our political leaders don't adequately focus on the important social issues that are of national common cause.

The truth is, we haven't elected a president by a majority of voters in this country in sixteen years. The last presidential election produced the first contested result in 130 years, and the popular vote was the closest in four decades. Now likely-voter registration is equally divided between Republicans and Democrats, and that division suggests that this year's election could be as close as the last. To say we're a people without broad national consensus is a wild understatement.

But our political parties and our politicians in Washington have managed to form at least one profoundly important consensus. Most of our elected officials, whether

Republican or Democrat, have decided that whatever is good for big business is good for America. Never have government and big business been in a tighter embrace. Certainly not fifty-two years ago, when General Motors chairman Charles Wilson told senators during his confirmation hearings to become secretary of defense that "I thought what was good for the country was good for General Motors and vice versa." Most of today's CEOs strongly emphasize the "vice versa" and rarely bother to echo the first part of Wilson's sentence. Wilson was hardly the shy, retiring brand of capitalist, but his statement was relatively mild compared to the Fiorina declaration of ruthless capitalism. It makes you wonder, if Fiorina thinks there's no right to a job, what other rights would she have us surrender in order for her and other CEOs to drive up quarterly profits and their companies' stock price? Would it make it less strenuous for our overstressed yet highly compensated CEOs if we were to repeal OSHA and workmen's compensation? How about getting rid of those burdensome clean air and water laws? Do we really need those silly child labor laws?

I wish I could tell you that Fiorina is part of a small minority in Corporate America, but she's not. Fiorina simply said out loud and straightforwardly what most CEOs are thinking when they pursue short-term profits with regard for nothing but themselves and their investors. Their employees, the communities in which they work, and, yes, the nation all fall by the wayside. And they are spending hundreds of millions of dollars to be sure that their self-interested message gets through to as many of our elected officials as possible: What's good for business is good for America. Business, industry associations, and lobbying groups like the Business Roundtable and the U.S. Chamber of Commerce concentrate most of those hundreds of millions of dollars on our congressmen and senators and their staffs in order to preserve the political gains of deregulation over the past quarter century and to promote the orthodoxy of free trade, including the outsourcing of jobs to cheap foreign labor markets, no matter what the pain to American workers.

The Business Roundtable is a prominent special-interest group that represents the CEOs of many of America's largest and best-known companies. Based in Washington, the Roundtable is a powerful organization that looks after the needs and wants of those CEOs, especially when it comes to influencing politicians. The Roundtable usually limits its activities to getting the right people into the right offices and making sure that the voices of its member CEOs are heard loud and clear on Capitol Hill. The Roundtable seldom attacks anyone publicly, but they made an exception for me and my adamant commentary against the practice of shipping those jobs overseas.

In late April, Roundtable executive director John Castellani devoted an entire speech in front of the Detroit Economic Club to what he called the "Myth of Outsourcing." As I read the wire service reports, I wondered first what Castellani and the Roundtable would consider a myth. Why would Castellani devote an entire speech to something he considered a myth? Then came the personal attack against me. Referring to the fact that I am a lifelong Republican and a strong believer in the relationship between free enterprise and democracy, Castellani said, "It's as if whatever made Linda Blair's head spin around in *The Exorcist* has invaded the body of Lou Dobbs and left him with the brain of [Democratic presidential candidate] Dennis Kucinich."

I laughed out loud. Not exactly a belly laugh, but a strong chuckle at least. It was a good line. But he wasn't being original. Daniel Henninger of the *Wall Street Journal* had written those same words in his brilliantly crafted op-ed column attacking me two months earlier.

Then, at a press conference after his speech, Castellani went original and came up with his own word to describe my opposition to outsourcing. He described my commentary against outsourcing as a "jihad." This reference to terrorism, inadvertent or not, also made its way into an editorial in *The Economist* magazine that accused me of embarking "on a rabidly anti-trade editorial agenda" and "greeting every announcement of lost jobs as akin to a terrorist assault." The fevered language in the media only served to clarify for my viewers and readers that something new and decidedly peculiar was going on here. I had obviously annoyed the establishment. The "Orthodoxy of Thought" was mortally offended by my temerity in questioning business practices and public policy that in my opinion fail to reflect the best interests of working men and women, the middle class, and the country. The viewers of my broadcast and readers of my columns know I've never called for a boycott of companies that outsource American jobs, never called CEOs who've engaged in the practice any nasty names, or suggested at any time that the United States should be protectionist.

Why, then, did Gerard Baker, in his *Financial Times* column, describe me as the "high priest of demotic sensationalism"? Could it be because Baker had no other basis to attack what I've been saying than to make it personal? Could it be because Baker and the others might have to question their own thinking about the role of business in America and—God forbid—the responsibility of business leaders that goes well beyond a financial statement and stock price? After three decades in television news and straightforwardly telling it the way I see it, I'm used to people taking a shot at me from time to time. I've been accused of not being objective in my reporting because I wear a flag pin on my lapel, in honor of those who were killed on September 11. The *New York Times* published an article that charged me with the heinous offense of calling the United States "the greatest democracy in the world" on the air, after the September 11 terrorist attacks. I was criticized by some in the media for saying the war on terror should be called what it is, namely, a war against radical Islamists. Those critics and the White House found common ground on that issue: The White House refused to let Condoleezza Rice come on my show after I criticized the Bush administration for not saying the name of our enemy in the war on terror. One of my producers says, now that I'm criticizing outsourcing of jobs, that I've moved from persona non grata at the White House to enemy of the state.

I've always managed to offend the sensibilities of both Republicans and Democrats. But this time, many Democrats and most Republicans are angry with me at the very same time. And a good number of CEOs are furious. When attacked so energetically and so personally, I have to admit, it does make a fellow think. After all, I've criticized Corporate America before, taking CEOs to task for their egregiously excessive compensation, bad governance, and the need to expense stock options. For more than two years, ever since the corporate corruption scandals began, we've carried a Corporate America Criminal Scoreboard as a nightly element of the broadcast. What's different this time? The answer, of course, can be summed up in two words: "Exporting America."

Since early 2003 on my CNN show, *Lou Dobbs Tonight,* we've run regular reports called "Exporting America," and I've been criticizing the outsourcing of American jobs in my columns in *U.S. News and World Report* and the Tribune Syndicate. The shipping of American jobs to cheap foreign labor markets is something I obviously consider to be one of the biggest problems facing the United States today. Quite simply, the problem is that more and more American companies, and even government agencies, are sending American jobs overseas purely to cut costs. In the process, however, we are losing high-quality jobs in this country by the thousands every month. Jobs that were once filled by American workers—whether blue-collar factory workers or white-collar professionals—are now being performed by people in other countries for a fraction of the pay that Americans used to take home.

And I don't think we're getting those jobs back. At least not until our business and government leaders decide to do something about it, or they're forced to do it out of political necessity or crisis. Even then it won't be an easy task, because many of them truly believe that outsourcing of American jobs is just a routine part of competing in a global economy, that the number of jobs lost relative to the entire U.S. workforce is simply irrelevant, that outsourcing to cheap labor markets is the only way the United States can be competitive, or, even worse, as the president's chief economist has said, that outsourcing is good for America. Either they don't comprehend that outsourcing threatens our economy, our jobs, and our way of life, or they choose not to comprehend or care.

Getting many CEOs and politicians to understand this is going to be tough because they simply don't believe that anything or anyone should interfere with their almost ecclesiastical views of the political economy. Or rather, they believe so fervently what is easiest for them to believe: that the great "Market god" in its wisdom and with its great, sweeping invisible hand will ultimately deliver prosperity for others, and livelihoods for the deserving, so long as no one does anything to incur its divine wrath. Irresistibly, these business leaders act wholly in their self-interest, freed by the Market of concern for their employees, their communities and broad obligations to our society. And many—too many—of our elected officials in both parties choose not to annoy the Market, for Corporate America might be annoyed as well, and then the vast campaign funding that flows from big business might slow to a trickle or be directed to candidates who profess their unblinking faith in the Market. Allegiance and fidelity to free trade, opposition to regulation, and unfettered free enterprise are the basic tenets of the true believers, whether politicians, CEOs, or academics. They truly believe that in the long run, the Market will work things out for everyone. The true believers have apparently raised their faith in the Market from philosophy and theory to the level of religion and ideology. Intoxicating stuff, this blind faith in the Market. How else can one explain why big business and Washington ignore staggering economic realities like a $500,000,000,000 trade deficit and the fact that the United States has been unable to run a trade surplus for the past twenty-eight years? How can any reasonable person ignore the fact that the United States is a debtor nation, desperately dependent upon foreign capital to finance not only our record trade deficits but also our record high federal budget deficits and staggering household debt that is putting an unprecedented burden on all American workers and their families? And now Corporate America, with the help of political leaders who are allied with them, wants us all to believe that the way to compete in the world is to ship American jobs to the lowest-paid foreign workers? Frankly, if our corporate leaders had demonstrated greater success in global competition, I might be far more inclined to take some of their views more seriously. But as I see it, they are outsourcing jobs because they and their corporate enablers, consultants like Accenture and McKinsey, are simply fresh out of new ideas. And working men and women are paying the price.

It's been almost three years since the end of the 2001 recession. Despite strong growth, the American economy has only just begun to create jobs, and those jobs, in the main, aren't the high-paying, high-value jobs typically created in recovery from a recession. Our trade deficits and budget deficits are soaring, together amounting to a trillion dollars a year. Even with solid economic growth and outstanding corporate earnings, good jobs aren't being created at a rate sufficient to keep up with population growth.

Those outstanding corporate profits are the result of higher productivity, and at least part of the credit for that improvement should go to the American worker. For the past several years, business has pushed fewer employees to work longer hours to produce more—and often without additional compensation. According to the Economic Policy Institute, the average American worker has added 199 hours to a year's work since 1973. Since companies began shedding jobs during the recent economic downturn, employees who remained behind are working more in order to avoid being the next victims of a cutback.

Business, shell-shocked from the 2000 market collapse, the recession of 2001, and September 11, continued to lay off workers long after the recession ended, and delayed any substantial hiring as long as possible. It appears that hiring has begun in earnest. Let's hope so. Yet the outsourcing of well-paying American jobs to cheaper overseas markets is not only continuing but accelerating. A recent Ernst & Young survey shows that most businesses intend to increase their outsourcing by half next year. Why? Corporate America's answer is to generate "higher productivity," "more efficiency," and "greater competitiveness." But those terms, as good as they sound, are usually simply code words for "cheaper." "Cheaper" doesn't have quite the same ring, does it? The code words are used to cover the exportation of good American jobs to countries like India, China, Romania, and the Philippines—countries that are wonderfully free of environmental and safety regulations. Such regulations would, of course, interfere with the efficiency and productivity of their labor forces, who in some cases toil for less than a dollar an hour.

The corollary to Corporate America's assertion that it must outsource American jobs to achieve greater global competitiveness is draconian: Big business is saying that all we need to do to become the most competitive nation on earth is to cut wages, throw out our environmental, worker safety, investor protection, product liability, and consumer laws, and eliminate corporate tax obligations altogether—and while we're at it, let's repeal those unfriendly antitrust laws. There's no doubt the result would be sharply lower wages and higher profits, but the result would also be a plummeting standard of living and the shattering of the American dream.

The managements of hundreds of our largest companies obviously don't share the American dream. Or they believe that because their companies are U.S. multinational corporations, they have less—or no—responsibility to preserve that dream. They seem to think that their businesses are, first and foremost, international companies, not American. Otherwise they couldn't routinely ignore the needs of their employees and their communities and outsource their jobs to lower-paid workers in other countries.

The exportation of American jobs abroad is a relatively recent phenomenon in our history. But in the course of the past thirty years, we've lost millions upon millions of manufacturing jobs, and our CEOs, economists, and policy makers—Democrat and Republican—have assured us that all this is the inevitable result of postindustrial, modern economies, both advanced and developing, seeking comparative advantage, which will result in a higher standard of living for all of us.

It is worth noting that our policy makers' assurances have largely been based on the research, study, and influence of powerful business lobbyists, who typically have been more than a little indifferent both to the welfare of the American economy—in which they themselves are based—and to the labor market, which also happens to be the principal component of what is by far the world's richest consumer market.

We are now witnessing the exportation of high-value jobs in information technology, financial services, law, and engineering to low-cost labor markets all over the globe. Corporate CEOs and many private economists (called "private economists" because in most cases they are in the employ and pay of private businesses, usually large multinational corporations) speak glibly about the blessings of higher productivity, the importance of efficiency, and the holy grail of global competitiveness. It's almost reached the point at which it all sounds like a mantra, at least to those us who are not "true believers."

Despite what Corporate America is suggesting, American workers are productive—in fact, the most productive in the world. They aren't failing to compete with workers in any part of the global economy. The truth is, American workers aren't being asked to compete; U.S. multinationals are asking them to give up their standard of living and their quality of life, or else.

Forrester Research estimates that $151.2 billion in wages will be shifted from the United States to lower-wage countries by 2015. That includes about 3.4 million white-collar service jobs. Interestingly, the sector leading the way will be the information technology industry. There's a cruel irony at work here: No one batted an eye when we moved manufacturing jobs out of the country, because we were sure those jobs would be absorbed in the services sector—specifically, the information technology industry.

Some jobs are sent overseas routinely: back-office accounting and call center work such as customer calling and customer support. But over time, according to Forrester, even jobs that require higher skill sets will be sent to other countries. These include professional jobs in areas such as architecture, life sciences, law, and business management. Forrester thinks that roughly 550 of the 700 service job categories in the United States will be affected by outsourcing in the coming decade.

It's not just corporations that are sending these jobs overseas. Many state and local governments are following the pathetic example set by Corporate America. And the trend is expected to worsen. A recent study by Input Research found that the market for state and local government information technology outsourcing will grow from $10 billion in 2003 to $23 billion in 2008. The problem now, however, is that some state and local governments are not simply outsourcing jobs to contractors that employ American workers. Several government agencies have actually begun to outsource work to firms that utilize cheaper foreign labor.

Forty state governments are now outsourcing what were American jobs. The state of Indiana's Department of Workforce Development is responsible for helping out-of-work Indiana citizens find jobs. Ironically, the department awarded a $15 million contract to update its computers to the Bombay firm Tata. The project would have provided employment to sixty-five workers coming from India on L-1 visas. The reason given for the move was the millions in tax dollars it would save the taxpayers of Indiana.

But the taxpayers of Indiana, like most of us, would have preferred that their tax dollars be used to help those out-of-work Indiana residents find jobs. Only after a loud public outcry did the governor of Indiana cancel the contract.

That such a deal was even cut is, of course, the worst kind of shortsighted thinking. People who don't work don't pay taxes. And if American companies are paying a worker overseas to do a job, that foreign worker is not paying taxes in this country. Keeping tax dollars here will continue to be crucial as states struggle to repair their finances. The Center on Budget and Policy Priorities found that weak tax revenues will contribute to the state budgetary shortfalls that will persist through at least 2005. According to the study, states will have additional combined annual budgetary gaps of more than $40 billion in 2005, on top of the $78 billion already reported for 2004.

Unfortunately, it's not just big business and the government that are compromising future American prosperity by seeking the cheapest foreign labor possible. Small and medium-sized businesses and professionals are also contracting out their call center work, telemarketing, and design and engineering work. The odds are high that a radiologist in India read and analyzed your last X-ray for your doctor and local hospital. And now a number of HMOs, insurance companies, banks, and credit card companies are processing your personal medical and financial information overseas. Of course, those countries don't have the same laws against the sharing and release of your personal information that you would enjoy had those records remained in the United States.

Those corporations exporting jobs to cheap foreign labor markets and exporting your medical and financial records are not only forfeiting American jobs and perhaps your privacy for short-term gain; they are also reducing tax revenues for local, state, and federal governments and adding to this country's trade deficit and current budget deficit. This has significant ramifications for our economy. Our trade deficit will continue to grow as we buy more from other countries than they buy from us, while our budget deficit proceeds on a runaway course as our government spends more money than it has.

With the importation of a trillion dollars of foreign-produced goods, we lose a trillion dollars of the U.S. consumer market. And we have no way to make it up, because there is no foreign market large enough to replace that trillion dollars. The result of the importation of foreign manufactured goods and the exportation of high-value American jobs is to dampen job creation, further erode our manufacturing base, widen our trade deficit, and worsen our position as debtor nation to the world. In economics, that isn't what they call a happy result.

At least not for us. It's a very happy result for China, Japan, the EU, Canada, the Philippines, Ireland, India, and a host of other countries around the world. Altogether, our trade deficit over the years, which also represents our insatiable appetite for those foreign goods and imported oil, has put three trillion American dollars in the treasuries and business accounts of foreign countries. True, much of that money comes back as investment in our financial markets, but those trillions of dollars amount to America's IOUs to the world. The world, in other words, now has a rightful and lawful claim of more than three trillion dollars on American assets. And their claims to our assets will only rise as our deficits widen.

For all the talk about global competitiveness and being the most productive labor force in the world, U.S. multinationals just haven't been able to sell as many goods and services abroad as Americans want to buy. Not only are we buying most of our goods from other countries, we're also increasingly buying back our services from other countries. The high-value jobs that are being exported to various countries around the world are not being sent overseas for the purpose of opening up these markets to U.S. products. Rather, those jobs are lost here, shipped there, and then that foreign labor works on the good or service for export back to the United States. The result: We're exporting jobs overseas to create goods and services that are then provided to this Great American Marketplace.

I am neither a free trader nor a protectionist, but I do admit to being extremely parochial in my view of globalization. My first and principal concern is the well-being of this country, and I'm sure it's yours as well. That is, unless you happen to be the CEO of a multinational corporation, or desire to be such, or you are a politician persuaded by powerful lobbying groups to overlook our national interest in favor of short-term profits for their clients, who see borders as occasional inconveniences.

Business groups claiming that outsourcing is good for the U.S. economy have simply gotten it wrong. They claim that jobs lost to exportation are simply transferred to new and emerging industries—that the displaced worker ends up in a new and equivalent job. As an example, the Information Technology Association of America (ITAA), which represents many of the high-tech firms that have been at the forefront of sending jobs overseas, published a report in March 2004 that, according to their press release, "conclusively demonstrat[es] that worldwide sourcing of computer software and services increases the number of U.S. jobs, improves real wages for American workers." The claim here appears to be that the more jobs we send away, the better off we all are.

Now, that is a breathtaking analysis and conclusion.

The fact of the matter is that the high-paying jobs lost in the recession are being replaced by work in lower-paying industries. Doesn't matter if you're a software programmer, a lawyer, or a medical technician—if your job gets outsourced, chances are that your next job will not pay as well as your old one.

It's time to begin questioning the current demands on our workforce and to talk straight about what higher productivity really means to our standard of living and what outsourcing really means for the job security and well-being of hardworking Americans.

The millions of unemployed workers in this country deserve better, and so do the millions of Americans whose jobs are threatened by mindless trade, labor, and immigration policies. Our government and corporate leaders need to come to terms with the new world in which we live, reject the domination of special interests and paralyzing orthodoxies, embrace fresh thinking, and demonstrate real concern for a people in need of a far more effective government. Either Corporate America must find a conscience and face the reality that life in this country is about far more than competitiveness and productivity, or all of us who care about this country and one another must demand that our political leaders represent the real interests of this country.

We might begin by reminding our business leaders and politicians that Americans want to be regarded as citizens, not just consumers, and that they need to see this great country of ours first as a nation, not a marketplace.

THREE

Working Against Ourselves

Wise are those who learn that the bottom line doesn't always have to be their top priority.
—William A. Ward

The exporting of American jobs has been a conscious and concerted effort by companies and their consultants to save money. In the rush to show Wall Street ever-improving short-term profits, companies have slashed payrolls and wages until there is little left to slash. They've found the solution to this seemingly intractable problem by replacing the existing workforce with a newer, cheaper version.

The corporations that have outsourced domestically for years, and the consulting firms paid to help them save money, took the concept to the next logical level: outsource abroad. Consulting firms like Accenture and McKinsey & Company were early adapters and enablers of the strategy. McKinsey created detailed analyses of how much money, down to the penny, companies can save if they opt for overseas labor instead of employing American workers. And while consultants deny that the outsourcing of American jobs is widespread, outsourcing revenue is the fastest growing part of their profits.

Businesses are started and run to make money—it's the essence of capitalism. But businesses also rely on their customers, employees, and suppliers, and that means there is also a responsibility to those stakeholders and not just to the investors. Despite their behavior, CEOs and their boards of directors are under no strict code of business management that insists that the profit margin is the only marker for a successful corporation. Listening to some CEOs, you might be forgiven for thinking that someone had absolved Corporate America of its social responsibilities.

In the past few years, the concept of corporate responsibility in too many businesses seems to extend only to senior management. Everyone else is on their own. Time and again in recent years, we've seen investors defrauded and employees laid off while CEO pay has skyrocketed. While wages in the United States have remained basically stagnant for the past three decades, CEO compensation has risen astronomically, now amounting to about 400 times what the average employee earns. Obviously, outsourcing offers an opportunity for management to make that ratio even higher.

Outsourcing, in the context I'm using here, is a fairly new occurrence. The term has actually been used for the past several decades to describe the process of subcontracting services such as data processing or centralized corporate functions. In particular, companies who found that they were straining to keep up with technological advances were "outsourcing" the management and maintenance of their computer systems to companies better equipped to handle them, like IBM and EDS. Outsourcers then ran the customer company's entire data processing division with their own staffs and resources, relieving the customer company of the need to build up core competencies it didn't possess, or to hire more staff with the necessary expertise. Outsourcing also relieved the customer of the cost burdens of benefits and pensions.

That was outsourcing ten years ago, and it also usually applied to staff or centralized departments such as back office accounting, or personnel and human resources.

Then came the term "offshoring," the building of plants and equipment overseas, often to provide facilities to bring back to the U.S. market products and services that were cheaper overseas. This has been done since the early 1970s, when high-tech firms sent the manufacture of their semiconductors, computer keyboards, and printed circuit boards "offshore." American companies built or financed factories overseas because countries

43

like Korea, Malaysia, Taiwan, Singapore, and eventually China were able to build large factories relatively inexpensively and staff them with cheap labor. Initially, many of those factories were built to create new capacity, because much of the primary manufacturing was still carried out by plants and facilities in the United States.

And of course, offshoring benefited U.S. companies in that they were opening these international markets by building plants abroad, which allowed them to compete with the locals in selling competitively priced goods.

But as American experts were sent to these overseas facilities to mentor their local managers and guide the foreign operations, there was a considerable transfer of the expertise and knowledge from U.S. shores to the factories of the Pacific Rim. It wasn't long before the Asian managers were as good as their American counterparts. And the outsourcing trend was underway, a trend that companies are capitalizing on today: With the transfer of expertise, knowledge, and skills, why not replace, wherever possible, expensive American labor with cheap foreign labor?

Several other factors were critical in the decision to develop offshore facilities. One, environmental regulations were all but nonexistent. This was especially helpful to companies that used or produced toxic chemicals in their manufacturing processes—which is to say, almost any company involved in producing computer components. Two, worker safety and health safeguards were similarly nonexistent. Many of the factory workers in Asia (with the exception of Japan) during the 1970s and '80s labored under sweatshop conditions. Those conditions still prevail in many countries, not only in Asia but also Latin America, although you tend to hear only about the ones producing celebrity clothing lines or athletic shoes. And third, these countries were essentially Third World economies, willing to provide financial incentives to almost any American company that would invest overseas.

These developments led to the broad exporting of American jobs when outsourcing and offshoring fused together. Show business and entertainment media were early adapters of the strategy. Popular animated cartoon shows like *The Simpsons* that were hand-drawn (not computer-generated) required a huge number of hours of inking and production to create a single episode. Producers of *The Simpsons* and other cartoons such as *Rugrats* found that Korean companies had for years been doing this type of production for animated shows originating in Japan. The Koreans had built-in expertise, and, of course, their labor costs were minimal relative to the costs of paying Americans. Soon, the scripts and storyboards that were generated in Hollywood studios were shipped over to Korea for full animation and production.

Other jobs, such as payroll and accounting, were

among the first to be shipped overseas to take advantage of cheap labor. After all, payroll isn't a specialized task, and the same data tends to carry over from month to month. Cheap foreign labor performing essential corporate functions was the hallmark of initial outsourcing.

Bangalore, India, arose as the center of a huge amount of this work. This city of 5 million was teeming with well-educated, skilled, English-speaking professionals. In the 1990s, Bangalore and other cities, such as Bombay, worked at a feverish pace to set up offices with high-speed telecommunications lines that could communicate at a moment's notice with customers anywhere in the world. And one of the beautiful things about Bangalore, from a corporate perspective, was its time zone. Bangalore is on the other side of the world, and its twelve workable hours coincide with our nighttime. Work sent to Bangalore at the close of business in New York could be performed all night and be ready and waiting on those same New York desks when the offices reopened in the morning.

The Y2K bug scare propelled outsourcing ahead. It was feared the shortcuts made in computer programs over the past four decades would destroy the world's computers because there had been no provision for inputting the year "2000," and organizations all over the world rushed to have their codes upgraded or checked so that their computers wouldn't fail in the new millennium.

There was a lot of work to be done and a lot of software to be checked. Y2K compliance threatened to overwhelm nearly every organization that depended on computers. To handle the colossal task at hand, programmers in Bangalore were hired to help out. The software was sent to them over phone lines and the Internet, worked on, and then sent back—all while America slept. In a matter of a couple of years, Bangalore found itself the high-tech capital of the Asian subcontinent.

The Y2K meltdown was avoided—although not everyone is convinced it would have been inevitable, by the way—and the small enterprises in Bangalore were ready for more work. The employees of these companies were educated, spoke English, and had demonstrated their technical expertise. And they worked for a tenth of the pay that American programmers earned.

Corporate America raised its eyebrows, focused on the bottom line, and signed on. Today more than 1,000 companies outsource their business processes and technology maintenance needs to Bangalore. The city has an estimated 150,000 programmers, and American companies are paying many of them. The best are living very well, on salaries of about $10,000 to $20,000 a year. In the United States, that's just about the poverty threshold for a family of four.

We've reached a point in outsourcing and offshoring where Corporate America is doing more than paying the salaries of Indian workers who handle data processing, or hiring a Malaysian company to balance the general ledger, or using a Taiwanese company to handle excess manufacturing needs. Companies are now exporting actual American jobs, jobs that can be identified and aren't just part of a general trend toward exploiting global consumer markets.

Why should we be so concerned about this now? After all, jobs and businesses have always moved—sometimes across town, sometimes across the state, sometimes across the country. Time Warner CEO Dick Parsons recently told me that he thought outsourcing to other countries was simply part of a business evolution that's been going on for decades. When he worked for then–New York governor Nelson Rockefeller in the 1970s, they were trying to keep New York companies from moving their operations to low-cost, nonunion states like North Carolina. Parsons's role in that effort was commendable, but the equation has changed dramatically over the years. The rise of multinational corporations has transformed what was once a competition between states—which had a positive effect on the national economy—into an unfair competition with low-cost labor in other countries. Of course, workers in North Carolina still pay taxes to the U.S. government, which ultimately benefits all of us. Cheap foreign labor neither pays U.S. taxes nor contributes to Social Security.

Technology has played the central role in outsourcing overseas. The so-called death of distance means that it now takes less time to move goods, services, capital, people, and information from one place to another. This phenomenon has been spurred on by a number of mechanical and technological innovations, beginning with the transcontinental railway and the use of steamships by immigrants. They moved people and jobs from Europe to the United States, and from the East Coast to the West Coast. In the 1950s and '60s, the national highway system and commercial air traffic cut distances, making the movement of people and products even easier.

Then came the high-tech drivers of the 1980s, including improved phone service, FedEx, and the fax machine. These allowed documents and data to be transferred in time that was measured in minutes or hours rather than days or weeks.

But the most important driver of modern change has obviously been the Internet. The seemingly real-time transfer of data over the Internet, from files and film to audio and video, has removed almost every remaining barrier to doing business in real time with anyone else on the planet. With the high-speed Internet connection, it's arguably easier to have someone halfway around the world review a document by e-mail than to get up and walk down the hall to talk with another person in the same office.

This "death of distance" has created an alternative network of workers around the world. That global labor pool has also created a disconnection between American companies and their American workers. A still small, but increasing, number of American workers telecommute or have flex time; they aren't in the office from eight to five, as they were ten or twenty years ago. Contact between workers and management occurs more often via e-mail and telephone and less often in person. From management's perspective, then, what's the difference between an American worker telecommuting from his home in the next town over and an Indian worker telecommuting from the other side of the globe? The result is still the same, isn't it? Hardly. The cost to the corporation is the biggest difference, and the American worker will always lose any global contest decided by the price of labor.

The central question is this: Should American workers be forced to compete for their jobs—providing goods and services to the American market—with workers in countries like India and China who make a fraction of U.S. wages? I believe the answer is "absolutely not." As much as I admire what the Chinese and Indians are achieving, I'm not one of those who believe in "trade as aid." For most of the workers in those countries, the increase in the standard of living that they earn from an outsourced American job elevates them to the upper middle class of their societies. Netscape cofounder Marc Andreesen, who now runs an outsourcing business, said to me on the show last year that building up the Indian middle class was one of the benefits of outsourcing. Now, Marc is a bright guy, but the fact is, we're jeopardizing *our* middle class if we continue this dangerous trend. I'd much prefer that CEOs look to their obligations to American workers and end outsourcing, instead of rationalizing what is simply a cost-cutting measure.

And I'd certainly prefer that our government look to the risks of one-sided "free trade" agreements that have resulted in a flood of imports into the United States. Incredibly, the federal government hasn't developed data about how these so-called free trade agreements affect American companies and American workers. We do know we have a half-trillion-dollar trade deficit. And we know we have to borrow hundreds of billions of dollars to finance our consumption of those imports.

Fifteen years ago Congress mandated economic as well as environmental impact statements on domestic policies but failed to extend the requirement for such research into foreign policy and international trade. In my opinion, Congress should do so, and soon.

FOUR

Globalization

No foreign policy, no matter how ingenious, has any
chance of success if it is born in the minds of a few and
carried in the hearts of none.

—HENRY KISSINGER

There was a time when a major corporation was defined by the country in which it was founded and did business: in Japan, companies like Sony, Toyota, and Mitsubishi; in Germany, Siemens and Mercedes. Companies like General Motors, IBM, and Coca-Cola were icons of American ingenuity, innovation, and competition. These giant corporations were emblematic of national spirit, strength, and global competitiveness.

Today many American multinational corporations seem to try to transcend their place of origin. They act as though they've grown so large as not to require a home country—they are "multinational" in every sense of the word. And the very term seems to mean they care little about the needs of the nation. In fact, their scale and size make them almost sovereign states unto themselves, and too many of them behave as though there were no national or community obligations.

As their power and financial strength have risen, U.S. multinationals have increasingly used their sheer mass to affect the political agenda. In my opinion, the multinational companies are now far too influential in American politics. These companies pay out hundreds of millions of dollars a year to lobby our elected officials. And they aren't paying those high-priced lobbyists to make sure your interests and mine are well considered by Congress.

Corporate interests spend more money on lobbying than the federal government's allocation for staff in Congress. One of the results of this inequity is that business lobbies, as well as the various institutes that are business-supported directly and indirectly—the American Enterprise Institute, Heritage, Cato, and Brookings, to name a few—generate more research and more sources for the political debate and legislative decisions than the government generates on its own. The effect is that big business all but controls the knowledge base upon which Congress usually makes decisions affecting economics and business. Ours, of course, is a political economy. Economics and politics are intertwined and inseparable in our way of life. Our representative government is still making choices for us, but lobbyists are, to an ever-increasing degree, influencing the options available to Congress. Which has the greater power is arguable; that the people have less choice as a result is inarguable.

Multinationals and their lobbyists have pushed through trade agreements that have contributed not only to the exporting of American jobs but also to the tremendous trade deficits we've run up for almost three decades. The Bush and Clinton administrations defined "free trade" as "give the multinational corporations whatever they want." Most pro–free trade organizations are funded by corporations, business or industry associations, or private donors with an interest in making sure that free trade—the kind we're engaged in now—continues to provide unimpeded benefit to multinational companies.

How can our politicians call trade "free" when year after year we sustain runaway trade deficits and the loss of hundreds of thousands of jobs? There is nothing free about such trade. It's mindless but certainly not free. What would happen if we quit pretending that current trade policies are "free"? Would our policy makers then address foreign policy and trade issues with clear eyes and acknowledge that the global competition for natural resources and capital may influence the welfare of the nation?

Our political leaders (and, yes, the national media) tend to look at countries as disparate as Russia and Australia, or Poland and Brazil, in homogenous terms. We give the same weight to a crisis in Liberia as we do to one in the

Philippines, homogenizing differences in geography, population, culture, and politics, and in effect, too often dealing with the world as if there were no distinction between ready friend and potential foe. Is China a friend of the United States? Maybe. Is Taiwan? Russia? Pakistan? Syria? India? Egypt? Is it in our long-term national or political interest to trade with China or to spend those hundreds of billions of dollars in the Western Hemisphere? Or is it in our national interest not to spend those hundreds of billions of dollars on imports, but rather to preserve our national manufacturing base—even expand it—and create more jobs at home? These are questions that should be addressed in a national dialogue. We should insist that our leaders—in both parties—deliver the answers to these questions. The answers, in my opinion, will determine our economic future and the standard of living for generations.

As it stands, well-financed, powerful lobbying efforts have rendered Washington content to let multinationals have their way, all in the name of globalization. Corporations have overwhelmed governments in the borderless global economy. And corporate logos in many cases have more powerful symbolic importance than national flags. In part, that's because more than half of the 100 largest economies in the entire world are corporations. That's right, there are now more companies than countries on the list of the world's top 100 economies.

TOP 100 ECONOMIES

Country/Corporation GDP/sales ($mil)

1 United States 8,708,870.0
2 Japan 4,395,083.0
3 Germany 2,081,202.0
4 France 1,410,262.0
5 United Kingdom 1,373,612.0
6 Italy 1,149,958.0
7 China 1,149,814.0
8 Brazil 760,345.0
9 Canada 612,049.0
10 Spain 562,245.0
11 Mexico 474,951.0
12 India 459,765.0
13 Korea, Rep. 406,940.0
14 Australia 389,691.0
15 Netherlands 384,766.0
16 Russian Federation 375,345.0
17 Argentina 281,942.0
18 Switzerland 260,299.0
19 Belgium 245,706.0
20 Sweden 226,388.0
21 Austria 208,949.0
22 Turkey 188,374.0
23 **General Motors** 176,558.0
24 Denmark 174,363.0
25 **Wal-Mart** 166,809.0
26 **Exxon Mobil** 163,881.0
27 **Ford Motor** 162,558.0
28 **DaimlerChrysler** 159,985.7

Country/Corporation GDP/sales ($mil)

29 Poland 154,146.0

30 Norway 145,449.0

31 Indonesia 140,964.0

32 South Africa 131,127.0

33 Saudi Arabia 128,892.0

34 Finland 126,130.0

35 Greece 123,934.0

36 Thailand 123,887.0

37 **Mitsui** 118,555.2

38 **Mitsubishi** 117,765.6

39 **Toyota Motor** 115,670.9

40 **General Electric** 111,630.0

41 **Itochu** 109,068.9

42 Portugal 107,716.0

43 **Royal Dutch/Shell** 105,366.0

44 Venezuela 103,918.0

45 Iran, Islamic Rep. 101,073.0

46 Israel 99,068.0

47 **Sumitomo** 95,701.6

48 **Nippon Tel. & Tel.** 93,591.7

49 Egypt, Arab Rep. 92,413.0

50 **Marubeni** 91,807.4

51 Colombia 88,596.0

52 **AXA** 87,645.7

53 **IBM** 87,548.0

54 Singapore 84,945.0

55 Ireland 84,861.0

56 **BP Amoco** 83,556.0

57 **Citigroup** 82,005.0

Country/Corporation GDP/sales ($mil)

58 **Volkswagen** 80,072.7
59 **Nippon Life Insurance** 78,515.1
60 Philippines 75,350.0
61 **Siemens** 75,337.0
62 Malaysia 74,634.0
63 **Allianz** 74,178.2
64 **Hitachi** 71,858.5
65 Chile 71,092.0
66 **Matsushita Electric Ind.** 65,555.6
67 **Nissho Iwai** 65,393.2
68 **ING Group** 62,492.4
69 **AT&T** 62,391.0
70 **Philip Morris** 61,751.0
71 **Sony** 60,052.7
72 Pakistan 59,880.0
73 **Deutsche Bank** 58,585.1
74 **Boeing** 57,993.0
75 Peru 57,318.0
76 Czech Republic 56,379.0
77 **Dai-Ichi Mutual Life Ins.** 55,104.7
78 **Honda Motor** 54,773.5
79 **Assicurazioni Generali** 53,723.2
80 **Nissan Motor** 53,679.9
81 New Zealand 53,622.0
82 **E.ON** 52,227.7
83 **Toshiba** 51,634.9
84 **Bank of America** 51,392.0
85 **Fiat** 51,331.7
86 **Nestlé** 49,694.1

Country/Corporation GDP/sales ($mil)

87 **SBC Communications** 49,489.0	
88 **Credit Suisse** 49,362.0	
89 Hungary 48,355.0	
90 **Hewlett-Packard** 48,253.0	
91 **Fujitsu** 47,195.9	
92 Algeria 47,015.0	
93 **Metro** 46,663.6	
94 **Sumitomo Life Ins.** 46,445.1	
95 Bangladesh 45,779.0	
96 **Tokyo Electric Power** 45,727.7	
97 **Kroger** 45,351.6	
98 **Total Fina Elf** 44,990.3	
99 **NEC** 44,828.0	
100 **State Farm Insurance** 44,637.2	

(*Fortune,* July 31, 2000. GDP: World Bank, *World Development Report 2000*)

These mammoth multinational corporations will likely grow even larger. Why? you ask. In order to be competitive in our global marketplace. Global competitiveness is the rationale for corporations whose scale would at one time have been unthinkable in the context of our antitrust laws. But these are not only American companies—they're U.S. multinationals. Yes, they are incorporated in the United States, where they enjoy the benefits of our capital markets and exchanges, and an increasingly unfettered capitalism—free of government interference—not found in any other developed nation. While the Business

Roundtable, the National Association of Manufacturers, and the U.S. Chamber of Commerce complain about the high costs of health care, lawsuits, taxes, and labor impeding their competitiveness, foreign competition seems to be having little trouble overcoming those burdens and competing in the wealthiest marketplace in the world.

Despite their complaints, American-based multinationals have managed to take advantage of our federal tax laws. Thanks to the foreign tax credit, the law is structured in such a way that companies are not taxed on profits that they can prove were actually earned in foreign markets. However, the tax code also allows for "deferral" of taxes on profits that companies consider to be the result of foreign operations. These taxes are deferred until such time as the company chooses to move those profits back onto the ledger in a way that they can be taxed by U.S. laws. The deferral should really be called a denial. As you've probably already figured out, that deferral can last a lifetime, because creative accounting will keep those profits from ever appearing as taxable income.

The deferral is one of the reasons that American multinationals move their operations to low- or no-tax countries. In effect, the government is providing an ongoing tax break to companies that move their businesses to countries that pay low wages. And the benefits don't stop there. Artificially shifting profits to these offshore or overseas operations allows companies to hide profits earned in the United States. Even though they should be taxable, these profits are hidden in corporate shelters and offshore havens that protect them from the hand of Uncle Sam.

How do they get away with this? Let's start with something called transfer pricing. The current tax law—specifically, Section 482 of the Internal Revenue Code—requires that companies set a price on every transaction between their U.S. operations and their foreign sub-sidiaries. In setting those prices, companies looking to avoid taxes will typically inflate prices on what the U.S. side "pays" the foreign side. Conversely, they will mini-mize the stated amounts that the foreign side pays to the U.S. side. The result is that U.S. profits look much smaller while foreign profits look bigger, thereby reducing taxes on both sides of the equation. It's a win-win situa-tion for the company, and a lose-lose situation for the U.S. government come tax time.

Then there's the transfer of assets such as trademarks to foreign operations. An American company with a regis-tered trademark or brand—considered a corporate asset—can assign the ownership of that to one of its foreign subsidiaries. In effect, this means the asset is not owned by an American entity. Such a transfer allows the foreign subsidiary to turn around and charge its American parent for the use of its own trademark or brand, all the while collecting royalties and fees. Of course, these royalties and fees are never physically collected; they are only virtual transactions—accounting games, really—but the parent company can claim that it is paying an actual dollar amount to use that asset. That amount doesn't get taxed.

But there are cases where multinationals do keep their dollars in the United States. It's just that this money often goes to endeavors that can be expensed and—you guessed it—not taxed. This includes paying for American-based research, facilities, overhead, and interest payments, most of which are exempt from taxation.

Finally, there's the matter of leaving it up to multinational companies to decide how they want to define their overseas operations. As part of a tax-simplification plan, the Treasury Department in 1996 allowed companies to take varying positions with different governments over the classification of individual operations. The law allowed the parent company to classify the operation in different ways, which meant that the company could call its operation whatever it felt like in one place, and call it something else in another place, and it was all legal. This was all done to avoid paying taxes—anywhere. If the foreign government where the subsidiary was based wanted to collect taxes, the parent company could say that it was a U.S. business—thus, no taxes paid to the foreign government. If the United States wanted to collect taxes, the parent company could claim that the subsidiary was actually a foreign-based company.

The Clinton administration, which had signed off on the initial tax plan in the first place, tried to close this loophole in 1998 once it discovered the way in which it was being abused. But backed by a significant lobbying effort, the GOP Congress prevented the Treasury from correcting the error. Democrats and Republicans worked together to sustain another benefit for American multinational companies.

Greed has overtaken a sense of higher responsibility to shareholders, to community, to employees, and to the public trust. Too many of these businesses are run with an indifference to basic American values and basic American responsibilities—like paying a fair share of taxes.

FIVE

The High Cost of Free Trade

*The budget should be balanced. Public debt should
be reduced. The arrogance of officialdom should be
tempered. And assistance to foreign lands should be
curtailed lest Rome become bankrupt.*

—CICERO

Incredibly, the proponents of outsourcing and free trade
will tell you that it's all a win-win proposition. It's been
my experience that you should reach for your wallet when
anyone says "win-win." Free trade and outsourcing are no
exceptions. There are winners and losers in our global
economy, and the scorecard is there for all to see. The
Commerce Department reports the U.S. trade deficit each
month. Germany, Japan, Russia, Canada, Brazil, and China
have enormous trade surpluses and are clear winners.
Turkey, Australia, Israel, Egypt, and the United States run
huge trade deficits and are clear losers. The United States
is the biggest loser by far. We've been losing for so long
that we're also the largest debtor nation in the world.

Free trade implies that trading partners achieve balanced benefits for their economies. That isn't even close to

being the case, unless you consider an annual half-trillion-dollar trade deficit to be close. You have to wonder how our business and political leaders can keep a straight face when they describe our current trade policies as "free trade." It may be free to them, but the cost to the country is exorbitant—and not only in dollar terms.

Free trade, in the minds of classical economists like Adam Smith and David Ricardo, is the exchange of goods and services that each trading partner provides most efficiently and productively and free of government interference, resulting in balanced benefits to both. But then, Smith and Ricardo could never have imagined anything like NAFTA and the WTO. It was under the mantra of free trade that the first Bush administration and then the Clinton administration entered into the North American Free Trade Agreement. The Clinton administration then signed on with the World Trade Organization, in which the avowed goal of all countries is to bring about a world of free trade. The result has been the deepening of U.S. trade deficits, a trade debt that has risen to more than $3 trillion, and a further erosion of American sovereignty.

Despite being the world's only remaining superpower and its largest consumer economy, we have failed to create and conduct trade policies that serve our national interest. In fact, we've been downright timid. President Bush's reversal of his decision to place tariffs on imported steel is illustrative of the confused thinking not only in his administration but in all of Washington. The World Trade Organization ruled that U.S. steel tariffs enacted by President Bush in 2002 violated international trade law. That decision cleared the way for the European Union to make good on trade retaliation threats against the Bush administration, and it chose a list of products to sanction that would inflict economic and political pain on the United States and the president. The EU cleverly but crudely targeted merchandise from states critical to Bush's reelection bid; notably, among the goods pinpointed were textile products from the Southeast, steel from West Virginia, and citrus from Florida.

Such sanctions are always designed to carry political punch, and who would have expected less from the Europeans? Apparently, the Bush White House. At first it appeared that the Bush administration would show some of its mettle. The president initially issued the steel tariffs in March 2002, not to alienate the EU but rather to save 150,000 jobs in our already decimated steel industry. There have been more than thirty industry bankruptcies since 1997, and many of its representatives credit the president's decision to put tariffs on steel imports with keeping the domestic industry alive. The EU and eight different steel-producing countries complained to the WTO, citing unfair trade practices.

It appeared that the president had decided he had a far more important constituency to serve than the members of the WTO, the EU, and the so-called free traders: namely, working men and women in this country. But the president blinked, and the tariffs were dropped in December 2003. Of course, Mr. Bush at the same time promised to fight illegal dumping and import surges, while claiming that potentially damaging sanctions against the United States had been avoided. In other words, the Bush administration declared victory in the midst of humbling defeat.

This tepid response by the Bush administration all but ignores economic reality and the national interest. Who has the most to lose in any trade dispute with Europe? America is Europe's biggest and best customer, and the U.S. trade deficit with Europe in 2003 totaled more than $80 billion. The United States has not run a trade surplus with Europe since 1992. For more than a decade the EU has sold the United States far more in goods and services than it bought. The global economy is absolutely dependent on the United States. This country carries an annual current-account deficit of $481 billion with the rest of the world. Ours is an $11 trillion economy, greater than the next five countries combined. Not only are we trading away our wealth while enriching other countries; our international trade policies are beginning to make

America look to the rest of the world like a gathering place for fools.

Today many of the Republican free traders I interview are quick to cite Ronald Reagan as one of their leading lights. And the Bush administration spent much of the spring of this year declaring the plants built in this country, and Americans hired by foreign carmakers to staff those plants, as proof positive that free trade works. The Bush economic advisors and cabinet secretaries continually call those plants and employees "insourcing," which they insist is an offset to outsourcing of American jobs. The administration has shown no shame at using this subterfuge, nor have the free traders shown any sense of irony in holding up these plants as emblems of free trade. The truth is quite the opposite: The Reagan administration took dramatic steps to force our trading partners to consider fair, not free, trade. The American automakers were hemorrhaging in 1981, due in no small part to the arrival of hundreds of thousands of cheaper and more fuel-efficient Japanese cars in American showrooms. They arrived in the wake of soaring oil prices in the 1970s. The Japanese had already been accused of dumping TVs and cars on America in the late '60s and '70s to gain market share. This, coupled with Japan's notoriously tight trade barriers, created anti-Japanese business sentiments in

Washington while American consumers were clamoring for Hondas and Toyotas.

At the prompting of the Big Three automakers, the Reagan administration got tough with the Japanese carmakers. The administration negotiated a "voluntary restraint" agreement—namely, quotas—with the Japanese, which essentially limited the export of their cars to America. This number was not to exceed 1.68 million cars shipped to America per year (increased to 2.3 million annually in 1985).

The Japanese realized that the world's largest consumer market was essential to their long-term success, but their domestic closed-door policy against U.S. exports now carried a penalty. The Reagan quotas meant that they either had to curtail their production and limit their revenue and profits, or find a way to succeed despite the limit on their exports to the United States. Under the quota system, foreign cars manufactured here and then sold here did not count toward the quota. It didn't take foreign carmakers long to decide to build here, hire Americans, and thereby get around the quotas. In a display of superior competitive strategy, Honda got a huge jump on its foreign competitors because it already had a U.S. factory in the works. When the quotas went into effect, Honda simply ramped up production in its Marysville, Ohio, plant.

Today the biggest Japanese automakers don't even meet their export quota to the United States because they sell so many of their domestically manufactured cars to Americans. And the American plants contribute the largest share of the Japanese carmakers' global profits.

Reagan's policy forced overseas corporations to make investments in the United States, from building factories to hiring American workers, if they wanted greater access to our market. The net result was positive for both sides. Foreign-based firms sold more products in America, while America benefited from the creation of new manufacturing operations and jobs.

Many free trade proponents insist that the Japanese built these factories in order to take advantage of the superior skill of the American workforce. Congressman David Dreier, a California Republican, is among those. While that goes against the facts, he's entitled to his opinion. However, Congressman Dreier and others who support the shipment of American jobs to foreign labor markets fail to acknowledge the irony of their views: If foreign carmakers are hiring Americans because of their superior skills, then why is Corporate America saying it has to ship American jobs overseas because American workers aren't as competitive or productive? The facts are these: The foreign carmakers built plants here and hired Americans because our trade policies forced them to as a condition of their having access to our consumer market. Corporate America is not exporting American jobs overseas to win access to foreign markets but to take advantage of cheap foreign labor.

In too many cases, American companies are building overseas factories and hiring cheap overseas labor, not to sell into foreign markets but rather to build products and provide services to the American market. In other words, we are permitting U.S. multinationals to do exactly what we won't permit foreign carmakers to do. If a U.S. company is going to sell into this market, don't you think we should insist on terms that are at least favorable to American workers and our trade balance? This isn't free trade; it's pure folly.

The Reagan administration took decisive action on trade, but that was more than twenty years ago. Today free traders don't even blink at our oversize trade deficit or the absence of a level playing field. This imbalance has been growing year after year, and now it's out of control. Yet, even as it became evident that the trade deficit was getting dangerously out of hand, it seemed as though no one in government or Corporate America was paying attention. The free traders and their supporters say it's all just the cost of doing business, part of globalization, part of the evolution of the international marketplace. Now our national policies are leading the United States toward diminished economic and political power, and unprecedented vulnerability to external forces that we may one day not be able to manage. And our government continues to negotiate trade deals without enunciating a clear vision of how our quality of life in this country will be affected.

One of the effects is America's rising dependence on imports. For instance, we are reliant on the rest of the world for our energy needs. U.S. imports of petroleum products have increased by more than 200 percent since 1970, with goods from the Persian Gulf now representing almost one-fifth of the crude oil products we import.

Moreover, net imports of petroleum are expected to grow from 55 percent of our total demand in 2001 to 68 percent of demand by 2025. A 1997 White House study found that improvements in the fuel efficiency of cars and trucks could reduce our oil use in 2030 by six million barrels per day. And one estimate from a pro-drilling group found that production from the Arctic National Wildlife Refuge could replace up to 70 percent of our imports from the Persian Gulf. But because our political parties view domestic production and conservation in purely partisan terms rather than in the national interest, we have done nothing to reduce our dependency on other nations to meet our energy requirements.

Our dependency on foreign resources extends well beyond energy. According to a study conducted by the Center for Labor Market Studies at Northeastern University, the United States is more dependent on immigration to meet its labor force requirements than at any time in the past eighty years. This dependency is principally the result of so many businesses being unwilling to pay a fair living wage to our native workforce to fill those jobs.

We should be worrying about the prospect of more jobs and more businesses being wiped out by cheap foreign labor, and even more worried about those who blindly advocate free trade for its own sake—well, actually, for the sake of powerful U.S. multinational corporations.

U.S. companies and multinational corporations operating in the United States pushed hard for the Free Trade Area of the Americas in 2003, arguing that it would open new markets for the United States' $10 trillion economy. But we'd heard this specious logic before—one decade and nearly one million jobs ago. Proponents of NAFTA declared that the 1994 pact would create 170,000 U.S. jobs annually.

Instead, at least 750,000 jobs were lost as a direct result of NAFTA. The Economic Policy Institute found that about four-fifths of those were in the manufacturing sector. When high-wage manufacturing jobs are replaced with service sector jobs that pay at least 23 percent less, the downward pressure on the wages of Americans is accelerated.

Free trade hasn't been entirely beneficial to our trading partners, either. NAFTA supporters predicted that Mexican workers would see increased wages, stemming the tide of Mexican migration. But Mexican manufacturing wages actually fell 21 percent between 1993 and 1999, and the number of Mexicans living in poverty now includes more than two-thirds of the population. As a consequence, NAFTA has stimulated illegal migration to the United States. Eight million to twelve million illegal aliens reside here, and more than half of them have crossed our southern border in the past decade.

NAFTA transformed a relatively manageable trade deficit with our neighbors into a full-blown problem. While U.S. exports to Mexico and Canada have increased by 57 percent, imports have risen 96 percent. As a result, the U.S. trade deficit with those two countries has ballooned from $9 billion in 1993 to $87 billion last year—and it's only getting worse.

The creation of millions of jobs during the 1990s masked the true detriments of free trade. But now that we can see the effects on our nation's workforce, economy, and quality of life, it is irresponsible of our government to pursue trade agreements as though there were no exorbitant costs for so-called free trade.

Here's what the modern application of free trade really costs: In 1951 the average U.S. trade tariff was approximately 15 percent. By 1979 the average industrial tariff sank to 5.7 percent, and now our industrial tariff on foreign goods is just under 3 percent. As a result, the United States has become the world's greatest customer on credit, accumulating a trade deficit every year since 1976—the cumulative total of which is a staggering $3.5 trillion. And countries like China, Japan, Germany, Canada, and Mexico are the primary beneficiaries.

Wal-Mart alone will import nearly $15 billion in goods this year from China. In fact, Wal-Mart as a single company is China's fifth largest export market in the world. Remember when the marketing message of Wal-Mart was "made in America"? No more. And it's not just Wal-Mart. Surveys show that Americans can't buy American even if they want to. The Economic Policy Institute estimates that 99 percent of our trade deficit comes from goods we now buy overseas because we no longer make them here. Seventy-six percent of consumers who look for American-made goods say they have a hard time finding them, and the reason for this is simple: We've given away our manufacturing base through "free" trade. At least 75 percent of toys sold in the United States are foreign-made, according to the Toy Industry Association. Ninety-six percent of all clothing purchased in the United States is now imported. Is that because foreign workers are smarter or more productive or have a better education or work ethic? No, it's because our principal trading partners have amazingly cheap labor costs. For example, the average manufacturing wage in China is 61 cents per hour, while the average in America is $16. Pursuing free trade policies that force the American worker to compete against third world workers with that kind of pay differential is patently unfair and absurd. It's actually surprising that we've lost only three million manufacturing jobs in the past three years. All for short-term profits for U.S. multinationals, and of course, all in the name of free trade.

Free trade supporters claim that globalization has brought us closer to our allies and lowered prices for American consumers. As Sheldon Richman of the Foundation for Economic Education wrote, "Any time we can have what we want at lower cost, labor and resources are liberated for additional things to make our lives better. We can have more for equal or less expenditure. Wealth is created. Remember this when you hear Lou Dobbs, Ralph Nader, and John Kerry trying to scare you." Sheldon is entitled to his view, but I think he's confusing liberating workers with laying off workers. It's not exactly liberating to lose your job to a foreign worker making a fraction of your pay, be retrained, and then have to take a job paying substantially less. I wouldn't presume to speak for either Nader or Kerry, but I firmly believe that we should all be frightened for our future. We are in desperate need of new thinking on trade, the fairness of current policies, and what kind of country we want our children to live in. At the very least, we need to begin to pursue a national policy of balanced trade.

Staunch protectionists believe we can turn back the clock and use high tariffs to protect every industry in this country. Their absolutism forces most of us to dismiss their concerns and even their valid points. But the absolutists who demand free trade should be dismissed every bit as quickly. It's time for all of us to realize that a purely ideological commitment to free trade is as foolhardy as absolute protectionism.

There is no more glaring example of the folly of unrestricted trade than China. The United States ran an almost $124 billion goods deficit with China in 2003.

I was the only American journalist to interview Chinese premier Wen Jiabao during his first visit to the United States, in December 2003. Premier Wen considered his trip here—and his meeting with President Bush—to be successful. But he told me, "We have to admit . . . in our economic and trade relationship problems do exist." Problems, indeed. Notice that the premier didn't say those problems were Chinese problems. The closest thing to a problem for China is the American demand that they abandon the peg of their currency, the yuan, to the dollar. (China pegs, or fixes, its currency to the dollar at a level of 8.28 yuan to one dollar. The result is that the yuan is very cheap right now, which keeps Chinese goods at extremely low costs in the international marketplace.) The dollar peg isn't a problem for the Chinese; in fact, it further helps to keep their exports to the United States cheap. No, the problem is that the Chinese don't like anyone, and certainly not the United States, to criticize their economic policies. Not only is our trade deficit with China likely to set another record, but thousands of high-value American jobs continue to be lost to cheap Chinese labor. No, the problems in the relationship are America's. By the way, China has again rebuffed the U.S. call to end the yuan-dollar peg.

Wen insisted that the rapid expansion of trade has benefited both countries. As you might expect, he suggests the solution is not to reduce Chinese imports but rather to increase U.S. exports to China. He told me, "We [should] seek mutual benefits and win-win results. We should look at the larger picture and larger interests of our trade for each country." And when we do look at the larger picture, and consider U.S. interests, we still have a crushing trade deficit with China, with no prospect of balance in the near future. In fact, China surpassed the United States as the most popular destination for foreign direct investment last year. And ten of China's top forty exporters are U.S.-based companies, such as Motorola. As I said, the problems Premier Wen acknowledged are American problems.

The relationship with China is emblematic of our relationship with much of Asia and Europe. Almost half the U.S. treasury bonds are now owned in Asia. Not only have we become dependent on Asia and Europe for goods and services—and apparently labor—but we are also now dependent on them for the capital to finance our purchases of their imports. It's hard to imagine how we could construct more destructive trade policies.

Whether it is the importation of petroleum or clothing and food, the exportation of jobs and manufacturing, or the foreign ownership of securities and bonds, America's dependency on the rest of the world has risen to dangerous levels. Successive administrations of Democrats and Republicans alike in Washington have been either unable or unwilling to confront America's rising vulnerability to external forces. Unless one of our political parties has an awakening soon and puts forward candidates that will alter the path this country has set for itself, we may well find ourselves confronted by circumstances we can't alter and events that we can no longer control.

SIX

The Exporters

*I see in the near future a crisis approaching that unnerves
me and causes me to tremble for the safety of my country.
As a result of the war, corporations have been enthroned
and an era of corruption in high places will follow, and
the money power of the country will endeavor to prolong
its reign by working upon the prejudices of the people until
all wealth is aggregated in a few hands and the Republic
is destroyed.*

—ABRAHAM LINCOLN

Cold Mountain, the best-selling novel about the Civil
War, was turned into a feature film in 2003. The film was
nominated for an Oscar for its cinematography and won
praise for its gritty depiction of America during the waning days of the Civil War.

But *Cold Mountain* wasn't filmed in America. It was
filmed in Romania.

The reason for filming in Eastern Europe was to save
money for the film's producer, Miramax. The film had a

budget of $90 million, but Miramax received more than $10 million of that budget back in the form of tax incentives from foreign governments for shooting overseas.

Gangs of New York wasn't filmed in New York, either; it was filmed in Italy. The TV movie *The Reagans* was filmed in Toronto, and *The Rudy Giuliani Story* was shot in Montreal. Classic American stories, with nary an American production in sight.

In 2003, of the eighty-eight American movies made for television, only five were made in this country.

We've been hearing and reading about filming done in other countries because of the costs of making movies in the United States. But it's now gotten to the point where the U.S. market share of movie production has fallen 22 percent in the past six years. Benefiting from that drop are countries including Canada, Australia, and New Zealand as well as Eastern Europe. According to the Film and Television Action Committee, that translates to about 20,000 lost jobs per year. This is hardly a reason to shout, "Hooray for Hollywood."

But film production is only one of a mind-boggling number of businesses that are cutting costs by going to other countries. It's one thing to think about acting and production jobs being sent to Canada or Romania, but what about medical technicians? Lawyers? Architects?

These are high-paying professional jobs that we've

always thought could never get sent overseas. We couldn't have been more wrong. Not only can white-collar jobs get outsourced, they already are.

We're accustomed, and almost immune, to the fact that manufacturing jobs have been disappearing in this country for decades. We've all heard the upside, too: how blue-collar workers are getting training and finding higher-paying professional—and white-collar—jobs after losing their factory jobs.

That scenario doesn't seem quite so optimistic when you realize that the white-collar jobs are heading overseas as well. If blue-collar and manufacturing jobs lead to white-collar jobs, where do white-collar jobs lead? Right now, they lead to low-paying wages in another country.

The truth is that we can't afford to lose either our manufacturing base or our professional jobs. If that happens, we will be in a position where we as Americans don't make or develop anything that we buy—which raises concerns about our level of dependence on other countries. We've seen how nasty things can get when the producers of oil decide to withhold their products from our country. Imagine if the manufacturers of our everyday items decide it's time to hold back on providing those goods to us, regardless of the cost.

Even though there are a huge number of people employed in America's service sector, we can't afford to allow jobs in those businesses to start eroding. Service sector jobs account for more than 60 percent of the employment in the United States, compared to 14 percent for manufacturing.

There are few places in the United States as emblematic of our service sector success as California's Silicon Valley, home to many of our biggest high-tech firms and some of our most skilled technology workers. But right now Silicon Valley is under the same kind of attack to which our industrial centers have been subject. Don't take my word for it. Here's a headline from *The Times of India,* dated January 6, 2004: SILICON VALLEY FALLS TO BANGALORE.

The newspaper boasted that Bangalore now has 150,000 information technology engineers, which it says is 20,000 more than are currently employed in Silicon Valley. And when you consider how many American companies are using services based in Bangalore, that headline may not be too far off the mark.

India is only one of the many countries benefiting from the exporting of American jobs. But it has also been one of the most aggressive in pursuing professional-level jobs, from medical technicians to software programmers. American companies have been all too happy to answer India's siren call of educated English-speakers willing to work at some of the world's lowest wages. For example,

General Electric's Capital International Services (CIS) was one of the pioneers in shipping domestic operations to India. In fact, it bills itself as the "largest shared-services environment in India." CIS now has four centers in that country, employing more than 13,000 workers, and claims to have realized savings of more than $300 million a year. The people there write software; they review invoices and insurance claims; they do market analysis. CIS also offers its services to other American companies looking for outsourced resources.

Let's look at several different job categories at the professional level, like those that Capital International Services offers, and describe what's really happening. Let's start with software programmers. There are programmers all over the world, but the Indian Institutes of Technology (known as IITs) are turning out thousands of these programmers a year. They are men and women who are well-educated, speak impeccable English, and are thrilled to make $10,000 a year. India's talents are not in manufacturing—it lags far behind other Asian countries in that respect—but it is no slouch in the services sector. That makes India well positioned to siphon off some of our highest-paying and most desirable jobs.

The high-tech industry is especially susceptible to outsourcing. With the exception of hardware, just about every aspect of the computer business can be outsourced. Systems software can be coded and debugged, applications can be tested and updated, and customer service can be handled anywhere a company wants to set up the necessary transmission lines. The high-tech industry, in setting up an infrastructure for transmitting its products, not only internally but also to its customers (many of whom now download their software directly from the vendors instead of buying boxed software and CDs), has also created a means for shipping its own jobs overseas.

Outsourcing is rampant in the high-tech industry, not only because of how easy it is but because of the desire to cut margins in a cutthroat business. As an example, IBM, once the biggest and most respected name in high tech, is now one of the biggest proponents of outsourcing. The company said in early 2004 that it would add an estimated 15,000 new employees during the year. At first it appeared to be a sign that at least one company was trying to fight the jobless recovery. Unfortunately, further investigation showed that more than two-thirds of IBM's new jobs would be based outside America. Only 4,500 of those jobs were slated for the United States.

Then IBM also said it would be shifting 3,000 existing jobs out of the United States. That means a net gain of only 1,500 jobs in America, with nearly 15,000 jobs going overseas, more than 10,000 of them newly created.

Asked about why this was being done, an IBM spokesman said, "We're doing it because there's growth in those areas . . . this is pretty good news for us and the industry."

The *Wall Street Journal* reported that IBM calculated the cost of an American programmer at $156 an hour, including pay and benefits. A programmer based in China was calculated to cost the company $12.50 an hour. Citing internal IBM memos, the *Journal* said that IBM advised managers who were told to break the news about overseas jobs never to use the word "onshore" or "offshore."

IBM called the *Journal* reports inaccurate, but I found them to be chilling. Those internal documents said it would be the job of IBM's human resources and communications people to sanitize the discussions of any moves offshore, so that the process would never be portrayed as a movement to cut costs or to export American jobs.

There are few companies as influential in this country as IBM. It is one that many consider to be both a thought leader and a leader in corporate behavior. Smaller companies around this country look to IBM for guidance in managing personnel and managing their businesses. So this kind of behavior goes beyond just IBM. We asked Sam Palmisano, the CEO of IBM, to join me on the show to discuss the ramifications of this. The company declined the opportunity.

SAS Institute, long known as one of the best companies to work for in the United States, and one of the largest privately held software firms, is now an outsourcer, so perhaps it will become one of the best companies to work for in India. Founder Jim Goodnight admits to being perplexed by the issue, but has managed to convince himself that it's more important for his company to act globally than locally. Goodnight told *CIO* magazine how corporate CEOs are managing to rationalize the process: "We are perplexed about what extent we should expand our operations in India. We've got about sixty people there now. With the price and the quality of the people, we're thinking, 'We really ought to do more of this.' But [then] there's that flag and country and all that stuff. We've lost our manufacturing jobs overseas; we've lost textiles; North Carolina is losing [its] furniture industry. I keep preaching that we've got to train our children to be knowledge workers. But guess what? That's what they're doing in India, too. And the Chinese are picking up on that as well—not only are they doing all the manufacturing, they're also getting into IT. So it's going to be a major decision over the next few years for every company how much IT should be overseas. We've already seen the migration of call centers . . . I think it's [offshore outsourcing of IT] a concern, but I don't know what we can do about it. This issue has been bothering me a great deal—about whether we should put more resources into our Indian operations or not—it's very perplexing. Then I was reminded that SAS is a global company. We're not just an American company, and we should put resources anywhere on the globe where it makes sense. I'm slowly coming around to the idea that we really might need to put more there [India] and less in the U.S." By the way, SAS is headquartered in Cary, North Carolina, U.S.A.

Goodnight has the reputation of being one of the most generous employers in technology, so when he has to struggle not only with outsourcing American jobs to cheap labor markets, but also with whether his company is American or global, we all need to take a step back, take a deep breath, and begin to think. Really think. About who we are and what this country is all about.

The high-tech offshore exodus continues. In 2003, Bill Gates went to India and promised to put $400 million of Microsoft's investment dollars into that country—Microsoft's single biggest investment outside the United States. One hundred million of those dollars will go to a development center that will employ 500 people, another $20 million to accelerating computer literacy in India, and the biggest chunk—$280 million—to development of, and training in, Microsoft technologies. *The Times of India* reported that Microsoft has contracts with more than

3,000 Indian companies, which employ some 250,000 developers. Those companies are developing products based on Microsoft technologies, and the paper estimates that work on Microsoft products constitutes nearly a quarter of the $8 billion worth of outsourced work done in India.

Intel, the world's largest maker of computer chips, claims that since 70 percent of its business comes from outside the United States, it's natural for the company to set up overseas operations. It's "just following its customers," according to CEO Craig Barrett. Addressing a crowd at an industry event, the Gartner Symposium Itxpo, Barrett was quick to blame the United States educational system and burdensome U.S. accounting and tax laws for outsourcing, indicating that companies were being forced to go overseas simply in order to protect their bottom lines. Yet his predecessor, the legendary Andy Grove, is not so sanguine. In fact, Grove has called for the government to help effect a balance between allowing businesses to provide shareholder value and helping them keep American workers employed. These contrasting views from the leader and former leader of Intel are all the more remarkable because it's a company that had to be saved from foreign competition in the 1980s—and a company that won a U.S. tax court ruling that allowed it to treat the sale of U.S.-made microchips as income from its Japanese operations, which meant that it paid no U.S. taxes on those products. However, Japan treats those same profits as American-generated and thus requires no tax, either. Intel ended up not having to pay tax on these profits—at all.

Ross Perot famously warned us about that "sucking sound from the south" as he opposed the creation of NAFTA. But the very companies he founded are outsourcers. Perot Systems is an IBM competitor and a huge proponent of sending jobs overseas. Its plans for 2004 included the addition of more than 3,000 call center and bill-processing jobs in India. The company also said it was creating two new facilities in that country during the year, which amounts to an investment of tens of millions of dollars. Downplaying the negatives, Perot said that this represented the company's purchase of Indian firms that already do outsourcing work. Despite the spin, Perot now has a substantial Indian operation involving thousands of employees—and I should point out that at the end of 2003, Perot Systems told my staff that it had sent fewer than fifty jobs overseas.

Perot Systems is now engaged in the kind of outsourcing that results in the exporting of American jobs. Ross Perot owns 30 percent of Perot Systems. He also founded EDS and was one of the first to bring the exporting of jobs to other countries to the national spotlight. Perot's warning about jobs going to Mexico was prophetic, of course, and hardly anyone thought he would be guilty of understatement. And no one at the time would have guessed that those jobs would also be heading in droves to India, the Philippines, Romania, Ireland, Poland, and various other quarters. And who would have guessed that Ross's company would be contributing to the problem?

The number of high-tech firms that outsource to India reads like a who's who of the high-tech industry: Apple, Computer Associates, Dell, Hewlett-Packard, Oracle, and Sun, to name just a few. Executives from some of these companies attended the 2004 Reuters Technology, Media and Telecommunications Summit in New York and said they will create more jobs in countries such as India and China than they will in the United States. I guess that shouldn't be a big surprise to anyone, but last year U.S. technology employment dropped to its lowest level since 1999. And, as *The Times of India* reminds us, technology companies outside the United States continue to boom.

While hundreds of high-tech firms in the United States are outsourcing, the trend goes well beyond the high-tech industry. Medicine, that most personal of professions, is already outsourcing. As health care costs increase, hospitals face the same pressures that our factories face: the need to reduce the cost of operations. Even in hospitals the search for the lowest-cost providers and suppliers invariably results in outsourcing. Many of the administrative aspects of health care, and certainly those involving accounting, have already made their way to countries like India. Everything from creating invoices for patient treatment and the processing of insurance claims to bill collection is routinely handled by Indian firms. Responding to concerns about health care outsourcing, many hospitals shrug it off because it doesn't involve actual patient contact or care.

But outsourcing is now part of the relationship between doctors and patients, a relationship held to the highest standards of privacy. Medical records and patient diagnoses, both real-time and recorded, are sent over communications lines to India. There, transcribers type out the doctor's words and send them back to the U.S. hospital. They can then be printed out as documents and inserted into the patient's medical file, all by the time the doctor begins his next set of rounds.

Massachusetts General Hospital, one of the country's most prestigious medical institutions, ignited a firestorm when it was learned that the hospital was sending X-rays and MRI scans to India for examination. The reading and interpretation of these images is the purview of radiology, a medical specialty that has some 30,000 qualified members in the United States. Apparently, hospitals think there are not enough of them or that they're overpaid. Radiologists, who routinely make upward of $250,000, are finding that Indian specialists are willing to do their jobs, in the middle of the night, at a tenth of the cost.

Mass General, a Harvard hospital often referred to as "Man's Greatest Hospital," is only one of the many American hospitals outsourcing pieces of patient care. These hospitals and many doctors claim that it takes too long to get radiology data back, because radiologists don't or won't work nights, and that there aren't enough of them to call on as needed. The American College of Radiology backs this up by saying that demand far exceeds the number of qualified radiologists currently produced by med schools.

Technicians in India aren't legally allowed to perform diagnoses on U.S. patients—they'd have to be licensed here—but they help sort through data, provide interpretation, write preliminary reports, and turn two-dimensional images into more easily readable 3-D images. Because of the time difference in India, they provide after-hours services during their day, which coincides with nighttime hours here.

Even though Medicare doesn't pay for work done

outside the United States, the hospitals have found a way around that. After getting the preliminary data back during the first hours of daylight, a licensed U.S. radiologist reviews the work and signs off on it. At that point it's all legit because an American doctor has signed his or her name to it. Medicare soon gets the bill.

There are a huge number of concerns here, not the least of which is, who is helping your doctor or hospital make decisions about your health and your treatment? Also, medical care is about as personal as professional contact gets, so it's of grave concern when you think that your records are being sent overseas to be handled by technicians or doctors who are not licensed—and not even liable—in the United States.

Yet radiology is only one part of medicine vulnerable to outsourcing. The reading of other documents, such as EKGs and EEGs, is an obvious next step. So is the analysis of tissue samples, which can now be digitized and read by pathologists. How about assigning medication based on the review of these and other medical analyses and diagnoses? That may not be too far behind. And as doctors and patients begin to embrace remote monitoring of everything from vital signs to pacemakers, who's to say that such monitoring can't be done overseas?

The privacy issues are significant. Few countries have the same laws the United States has that protect patients' rights and doctor-patient confidentiality. How do you prosecute someone in India who might choose to disseminate information about patients? Or use it for their own gain? If that sounds a little too far-fetched, then you should know that it's already happened. In 2003, the University of California, San Francisco Medical Center was subcontracting the transcription of doctors' dictation and various other medical records. The subcontractor outsourced the work to Pakistan. There, an aggrieved Pakistani transcriber, claiming she had not been properly compensated, threatened to publicize the medical records she was working on. She sent an e-mail to UCSF demanding payment, or else. The blackmail worked, and the woman was paid. The vulnerability is real, and there's absolutely no way for American rights to be protected.

But in an interesting twist, the legal profession is also at risk of outsourcing. And the reason is the same as everywhere else: to cut costs. Market research firm Forrester Research predicts that in the next eleven years nearly 8 percent of law industry jobs will shift to low-cost countries. Paralegal work and work done by junior lawyers is particularly vulnerable to outsourcing. Large legal firms, who pay young associates high salaries for doing lots of entry-level work, are looking for ways to cut costs. That can be done by shipping those jobs overseas.

The first wave that's headed offshore is those jobs that can be commoditized. Large companies such as General Electric and BorgWarner are sending out their corporate legal work, such as research, because it costs less than giving it to domestic legal professionals. The concern is that the more work that is sent offshore to contract professionals in places like India, the less opportunity there will be for young lawyers here to get proper training.

As with the medical profession, legal departments and law firms will probably send out the work normally done by paralegals, interns, and junior associates—certainly they wouldn't send out the work of highly paid partners. But one has to ask where less senior members of the staff will get their training if their work is being done on the other side of the world. These people, who often prepare drafts and do research, could be rendered unnecessary since senior partners usually look over these documents anyway. Their ability to do grunt work may thus become irrelevant if senior partners can save money by outsourcing it.

These junior law professionals, such as paralegals, don't approve legal documents, so the law profession says there will be no impact on the final quality of legal work. They state that any work done overseas and used here must be approved by an American lawyer, who is then

responsible for its contents. Having Indian legal professionals put it together is just a nice way to save time and
money for these attorneys. To help make it even easier,
some Indian firms are employing American lawyers to
oversee their output so that it passes muster before it even
gets shipped back to the United States.

Legal research and publishing have already discovered
the cost-cutting benefits. So what's next? A lot of people
would argue—and I would be one of them—that we
don't need so many lawyers in this country. But we do
need some, and we do need good ones. What happens
when the first tier of entry to the legal profession gets
closed off and shipped overseas? Will college graduates
still be willing to invest the years of effort and the many
thousands of dollars it takes to get a law degree? If they see
legal jobs outsourced, will they determine that they have
little to gain in an industry that puts less and less value on
their knowledge and skills? The way things are going, it
doesn't seem that we'll have to wait very long to find out.

There is, of course, another bastion of white-collar America that is taking a shine to outsourcing: the financial services industry. JP Morgan, Morgan Stanley, and Goldman
Sachs all have operations in India, where research is
turned out by financial analysts while Wall Streeters sleep.

The analysis is on their desks before the market opens in the United States. American Express has a center in Delhi running an international call center and processing credit card transactions. Number of employees: 2,000. E-Serve, a division of Citigroup, has workers in Bombay and Chennai. Number of employees: 3,000.

This is just the beginning for Wall Street, by the way. A.T. Kearney predicts that 500,000 financial services jobs will go offshore by 2008. Personally, I think that's a conservative estimate.

One of the complaints I've heard from thousands of our viewers is that when they call a financial services company or a technical support line, they find themselves talking to someone in India or another country. Yet the people on the other end identify themselves as Tom or Joan or John or Susan. Obviously, these are fake names employed for the reassurance of the American customer, who often has to struggle to understand what "Tom" or "Susan" is saying. Yet there is perhaps no other area of business that has been outsourced so widely as call centers, and it is the subject of the most complaints from our viewers.

Most of us have talked with call centers when we call an airline for a reservation or check on our credit card balance or need help figuring out why our computer software won't work. And more and more, these calls are going straight to India. The country has the largest English-speaking population after the United States, and it even has schools that teach native Indians to speak with American regional dialects, obviously with varying degrees of success.

Indian call centers started in the early 1990s, due in large part to the efforts of one man, Raman Roy. As an executive working with American Express and later GE Capital, Roy spearheaded the creation of India-based business processing centers for American multinationals. Building a telecommunications infrastructure and taking full advantage of cheap labor, he was able to save Amex and GE millions of dollars in labor costs in a few short years. Spurred on by his success with both companies, he ventured out on his own and founded the company that has become Wipro Spectramind, today considered the dominant player in Indian outsourcing, with revenues of more than a billion dollars a year.

The success of Wipro, Infosys, and other Indian technology companies is indisputable, and the most recent projections of Indian technology-sector growth are nearing $30 billion within the next few years. Entrepreneurial, and fully exploiting its low-wage advantage, the Indian technology sector is poised for continued global success. The fact remains that much of that success will be built on the transfer of jobs and knowledge from the U.S. marketplace. No one should blame the Indians for that transfer. The blame rests squarely with Corporate America and our elected officials, who either support outsourcing or ignore its impact on our workers and our economy.

———

SEVEN

The Myths of Outsourcing and Free Trade

All truth passes through three stages, first, it is ridiculed.
Second, it is violently opposed. Third, it is accepted as
being self-evident.

—ARTHUR SCHOPENHAUER

Gregory Mankiw is a lanky, bespectacled, low-key guy who looks the part of a former Harvard professor of economics, which he is. Mankiw has written a number of popular economics textbooks. He's also the chairman of the President's Council of Economic Advisers, and along with the president's economics adviser, Stephen Friedman, he has the greatest access to President Bush on economic policy. Mankiw, however, chose early this year to publicly support the shipment of American jobs to cheap overseas labor markets. He caused a brief outcry in Congress, and even the always loyal Speaker of the House, Congressman Dennis Hastert, was moved to separate himself from Mankiw's statement. Mankiw said, "Outsourcing is just a new way of doing international trade. We are very used to goods being produced abroad and being shipped here on ships or planes. What we're not used to is services being produced abroad and being sent here over the Internet or telephone wires . . . I think outsourcing is a growing phenomenon, but it's something that we should realize is probably a plus for the economy in the long run."

A number of people on Capitol Hill thought Mankiw should have resigned, but I disagreed. On my broadcast that night, I called on the president to fire him. Not merely because I obviously disagree with him, but because Mankiw's statement raised the administration's support of overseas outsourcing to a declaration of government policy. Now, maybe I'm being somewhat brittle about the matter, but I just happen to believe that our government should be on the side of American working men and women, not aiding and abetting the destruction of their jobs by supporting a business practice that even Mankiw said could "probably be a plus for the economy in the long run." Probably? It could also be a probable negative. It certainly is if you're one of the hundreds of thousands who've lost their jobs to outsourcing. When he added a further qualifier to his support by saying "in the long run," Mankiw kept his credentials as an economist in good standing. How long is the long run? How many jobs do we have to lose to outsourcing to determine whether it really is a "plus," or a definite negative? I invited Gregory Mankiw to join me on my show that night and a number of times since, to ask him those questions and to debate the issue, but he has consistently declined. The invitation is permanently open.

Mankiw spoke for the administration in his early support of outsourcing, and since then the Bush economic team has taken its advocacy of free trade at any price to new heights. The White House is not only making statements like "outsourcing is good for the American worker" but is defending its free trade policies by insisting that all of us who are concerned about chronic, bulging trade deficits and the outsourcing of American jobs are "economic isolationists." Really? I certainly have never called for protectionist trade policies, only fair trade polices. I've never called for an isolationist trade policy, only balanced trade. And frankly, I don't know anyone who has advocated any policy that could be honestly described as economic isolationism. And neither does the Bush administration. At a time when we should be having an honest, open dialogue about the impact of overseas outsourcing and free trade on American workers, the administration has chosen to indulge in rhetorical gamesmanship while ignoring the national cost of a half-trillion-dollar trade deficit, the huge quantities of foreign capital that we are now dependent on, and the emergence of a national policy that puts our working men and women in direct competition for employment with a third world labor force that will work far cheaper than Americans. There are a lot of misconceptions to address when we finally do begin that dialogue, and a lot of myths to dispel.

Myth No. 1: Outsourcing American jobs is good for our economy.

Even the chairman of the President's Council of Economic Advisers couldn't go beyond saying outsourcing is "probably" a plus for our economy, "in the long run." The problem is, there's no empirical evidence to support that position. We do know that workers who have lost their jobs to overseas outsourcing are finding new jobs that pay only about 80 percent of their original wages. And we do know that there are tremendous costs to the government to provide unemployment benefits and retrain these laid-off workers. Outsourcing may be good for the profits of U.S. multinationals, but that isn't really the issue, is it?

Myth No. 2: Outsourcing has improved productivity growth and the creation of high-value jobs.

Our gains in productivity have resulted from (1) improvements in business processes and operations as a result of the application of new technology, (2) employees who are lucky enough to have had jobs for the past several years and are working longer hours for basically static compensation, and (3) moving production and shipping American jobs overseas to provide goods and services to the U.S. market.

As for creation of high-value jobs, the numbers speak for themselves, and they are not encouraging. When the Bureau of Labor Statistics released its ten-year projections for American job growth in February 2004, seven of the ten biggest areas of job growth were in menial or low-paying service jobs. Here's the BLS projection:

1. Waiters and waitresses
2. Janitors and cleaners
3. Food preparation
4. Nursing aides, orderlies, and attendants
5. Cashiers
6. Customer service representatives
7. Retail salespersons
8. Registered nurses

9. General and operational managers
10. Postsecondary teachers

Only three of these job categories require a college degree. The rest rely on on-the-job training. These jobs of the future hardly qualify as high value.

Myth No. 3: Outsourcing is simply a part of free trade, and classical economists like Adam Smith and David Ricardo would have loved it.

Adam Smith believed that free trade allowed countries to concentrate their production on goods in which they had a natural advantage, and to acquire through trade other goods better produced by other countries. David Ricardo developed the concept of comparative advantage, which held that nations can benefit from free trade by concentrating their production on goods they can produce most efficiently, acquiring through trade other goods that permit them to concentrate on their comparative advantage and thereby enlarge their economy.

Smith and Ricardo did not envision a trade relationship in which there wasn't mutuality of benefit, that is, balance. Both economists assumed that national economies would act with a clear understanding of national self-interest. I strongly doubt that either Smith or Ricardo would be pleased to find their free trade theories being used to support the transfer of factors of production from developed nations to third world nations, to take advantage of all but limitless supplies of cheap foreign labor. They also could not have imagined that one nation would effectively risk bankrupting itself by transferring its comparative advantage of knowledge base, expertise, and capital to its trading partners, and then ship its jobs overseas as well. Our current trade policies aren't laissez-faire but rather "c'est la vie."

Myth No. 4: Our economy and consumers are strong enough to run large chronic deficits, and historically a trade surplus is a sign of a weakening economy.

This bizarre assertion was made by Congressman David Dreier—one of many he's made in trying to defend free trade agreements on my show. The dapper Republican congressman from California is the personification of the free-trade-at-any-cost philosophy, and unlike many in the Republican party, he has the courage of his convictions. The congressman is partially correct, to the extent that a trade surplus might occur when an economy weakens or goes into recession, and the purchase of imports declines. But the reality is that with our chronic trade deficits we are approaching $4 trillion in accumulated trade debt and must borrow foreign capital to buy foreign goods. As a result, our massive chronic trade deficits are clear evidence that our economy is not producing enough goods for domestic consumption and not producing enough goods that the world wants to buy or can afford. If that's not weakness, I don't know what is.

Myth No. 5: The only alternative to free trade is protectionism or "economic isolationism."

The free traders, within and without the Bush administration, have taken to casting the outsourcing and free trade arguments in terms of false choices: insisting that there is only free trade, as currently practiced, or no trade. But between the polar extremes of free trade and isolationism are a wide range of policy choices: In the center of the policy spectrum there is balanced trade. But Washington and Corporate America are opposed to balanced trade because it would mean a new direction in policy, a larger and more active role for our government, and an end to carte blanche for corporations in international trade. The real alternative to what we continue to permit Washington and Corporate America to call "free trade" is balanced trade, in which we negotiate trade agreements that are reciprocal in benefit—unlike the World Trade Organization or trade agreements like NAFTA. We have ten years' experience with the WTO, and we have eleven years' experience with NAFTA. That experience shows that free trade is not working for the United States. When one side—namely, the United States—is carrying a half-trillion-dollar trade deficit, it's clearly not benefiting us. Many of our biggest trading partners, notably China, are engaging in obstructed trade, yet our leaders keep insisting that it's free and fair. They state that this is the only way it can work, or else we become protectionist.

Well, the Chinese are protectionists, the Japanese are, and so is much of the EU. And they all have trade surpluses. Why should the United States not be able to achieve a surplus as well, or at least balanced trade?

Myth No. 6: Job retraining is the way to deal with outsourcing. Whenever industries and jobs have left our shores, we've retrained the workers for better jobs. That'll happen this time.

I think James Glassman, columnist for the *Washington Post* and an American Enterprise Institute fellow, answered this one just fine on my show. When I asked him what we would be retraining workers for, Glassman said, "One of the things about a dynamic economy is, we don't know what the jobs are." And that's the point. When you're exporting jobs that are at or near the top of what we consider professional careers, where is the next step up? How do you tell radiologists, lawyers, or architects that they can be retrained for better careers when they've already been to college, apprenticed, and interned and now are in desirable and well-paying positions? What are they going to be offered in the way of a better job?

When free traders like Glassman say, "Don't worry, we retrained blacksmiths after the advent of automobiles," they're talking about a move from one kind of production to a new one. We didn't just stop using horses and wait around for a better form of transportation—it had already arrived. That, however, is what's happening with outsourcing of American jobs. We're outsourcing high-paying service and professional jobs, yet there isn't a new job that is attracting labor, at least not in this country. Blacksmiths didn't lose their livelihood and then wait years for the introduction of the automobile. The automobile industry that forced blacksmiths and carriage makers out of business simultaneously created new jobs. Americans are not losing their jobs to a dynamic, rapidly changing economy. Americans are losing jobs because we permit U.S. multinationals to force American workers to compete with cheap foreign labor.

Myth No. 7: Outsourcing benefits everyone. Look at what happens when Honda outsources to the United States and builds cars here. The United States is insourcing as many jobs as it's exporting.

"Insourcing," as the Bush administration, the multinationals, and other free traders like to call the building of foreign factories in this country, is a sham argument. Honda, Toyota, and BMW, for example, built plants here to win access to the world's richest car markets. That required them to make an investment in American-based facilities and American workers. There is no similarity of any kind between the foreign companies' hiring of Americans to staff these "transplants" and the exporting of American jobs to India or other third world countries simply to take advantage of cheap labor, rather than enter a foreign market. The hiring of American workers in plants owned by foreign companies is not analogous in any way to IBM's shipping 10,000 jobs to India solely for the purpose of paying lower wages.

As I've mentioned, under the direction of the Reagan Administration, the U.S. Congress and U.S. trade representative forced import quotas against Japanese auto manufacturers after Japanese vehicle exports swamped our shores. The administration forced the building of plants by companies like Honda and Nissan and BMW in return for greater access to the world's largest consumer market. What the current administration and free trade proponents like to call "insourcing" is really just foreign direct investment in the United States.

Those foreign-based companies build here, and they sell here. They don't build cars here and then send those cars back to Japan or Germany for sale. They are building here to get access to our market, and they're doing a good job of it. On the other hand, our trade agreements rarely open up foreign markets to the degree that the United States has opened up its markets. We don't sell into those other markets, because we can't.

Myth No. 8: The goal of outsourcing jobs overseas is to increase productivity, not simply to cut wage costs.

Outsourcing proponents claim that it's all about productivity, not price. Almost everyone agrees that the American worker is the most highly productive worker in the world—and among the costliest. But for reasons of public relations, U.S. multinationals are loath to say they're exporting American jobs simply to cut their labor costs. No, instead they or their consultants say they're shipping jobs to cheap foreign labor markets to achieve "efficiency" or "higher productivity" or to raise their competitiveness. Nonsense. It's like the old saying: "When they say it ain't the price, it's the price."

To achieve lower labor costs, the U.S. multinationals are using their corporate consultants, such as Accenture, McKinsey, and others, to dress up the language and their rationale. And the consultants are being paid handsomely to do so. But the simple truth is that our multinationals and our elected officials who support them without reservation are callously and shamelessly selling out the American worker.

Myth No. 9: When Corporate America outsources jobs overseas, it enlarges its knowledge base and creates not only more jobs here but high-value jobs.

John Castellani, president of the Business Roundtable, said earlier this year, "Shifting routine computer programming, back-office, and call center jobs overseas does reduce the number of American jobs in those areas, but the cost savings generates new capital to finance the remarkable ingenuity of our economic system, to create new, higher-wage jobs here in the United States." That's the world we all wish we lived in. The problem is, there is absolutely no empirical evidence or data to support the statement. In fact, jobs lost are being replaced by lower-paying jobs.

Tom Donohue, president and CEO of the largest business organization in the country, the U.S. Chamber of Commerce, says that the United States also gains technical knowledge by exporting American jobs. Now, Tom is one of the smartest and most aggressive spokespersons for any cause or group in Washington, and a likeable fellow. But he's just plain wrong. Knowledge and expertise are moving from the United States to the cheap foreign labor markets along with our jobs. We're not only exporting American jobs, we're exporting our technology advantage.

Myth No. 10: We want to see countries like India prosper. Outsourcing helps their economies and their workers.

I really hope that none of the people who use this argument are suggesting that we create a middle class anywhere in the world at the expense of our own. Because for those who live and work here, for those who run companies based here, their first and foremost national concern should be the welfare of their own nation. As far as I'm concerned, there's no way you can help build your neighbor's house when your own is on fire.

Certainly we must aid other countries, but that doesn't mean we need to send our jobs to them at the expense of our own prosperity. The elitist one-worlders surely won't continue to demand that we consign our workers to an ongoing labor competition with China, the Philippines, India, Haiti, and Mexico. Those who claim that we have a higher responsibility to the world economy than to American workers might consider a visit to their local unemployment office to talk with a few of the people in the lines. Our highest responsibility is to preserve the American Dream for all Americans.

Myth No. 11: U.S. multinationals are outsourcing because Americans aren't well enough educated to fill the jobs.

First, it's simply untrue. The more jobs Corporate America outsources, the fewer workers to pay local, state, and federal taxes, which further punishes our struggling public education system. As Corporate America is fond of saying, companies don't pay taxes; people do. And if people don't have jobs, our tax base diminishes, and we have less to support public education. U.S. multinationals should be spending money, and setting up training for public school students, and volunteering to work in our schools, rather than lamenting the poor quality of education. In fact, we all should be doing far more to improve our public schools.

But the outsourcing of American jobs is worsening our problems, not solving them. The law of supply and demand will always determine economic choices. As Corporate America recruits more labor from third world countries, it is encouraging our young people to make educational choices that may be ominous for our ability to produce and for our future prosperity.

This past year enrollments in computer engineering jobs dropped 23 percent. MIT, arguably one of the most prestigious schools in the world, announced that enrollment in its engineering programs has dropped 33 percent in the past two years. Chinese schools now graduate more than 350,000 engineers every year, far above the approximately 90,000 who graduate annually from American institutions.

I hear some of the world's biggest technology companies bragging about the amount of money they spend on research and development. But they don't always make the distinction between R & D that's going on in this country and R & D that's going on in newly created facilities in other countries—facilities that house the labor that is replacing American workers. As we know, Microsoft pledged $400 million last year to create resources in India, on top of some $750 million it had already promised to China. That's more than a billion dollars that Microsoft has put into other countries while thousands of software programmers in the United States—still home to Microsoft—go looking for work.

Myth No. 12: U.S. companies have to compete in a world market. Even if everyone agreed that outsourcing is terrible, there's no way to stop it.

This is the fatalism defense of outsourcing. The multinationals say there's no practical way to end outsourcing. The reality is that we could end it tomorrow. Bruce Josten, executive vice president of the U.S. Chamber of Commerce, told me that the issue was complicated and that his members were still trying to figure out the ramifications, the laws, and the actual numbers of employees directly affected. I asked Bruce what he would think of a moratorium on outsourcing by Corporate America until his colleagues worked out the details with Congress and academia. Josten said he'd rather see Congress pass tort reform and rather we had a moratorium on politicians at the state level introducing bills to stop outsourcing. In other words, no moratorium on outsourcing—even though that would at least temporarily halt the practice and give us the time necessary to determine how many jobs have been shipped out of the country and how many more are at risk, and time to create a national policy on the subject. But of course, that's the real point: Corporate America doesn't want the public to know the real numbers, or the real impact, and the last thing it wants is— God forbid—a national policy on the issue.

All these myths and the facts that dispel them have been part of the early stages of a public dialogue, from the factory floor to the set of my show, from the floor of the U.S. Senate to the water cooler. Despite the extraordinary efforts of the multinationals, their lobbyists, and the politicians they support to distort the debate on the critical issue of outsourcing, I believe that nearly all working Americans understand that not only truth is being assaulted but also our economic future and our way of life.

———

EIGHT

For the People?

*A man willing to work and unable to find work is
perhaps the saddest sight that fortune's inequality exhibits
under this sun.*

—THOMAS CARLYLE

Many Americans who find themselves unemployed are often in need of government assistance. They use state-run programs, usually in the form of call services, where they can apply for and collect benefits over the phone. The states fund these services with taxpayer money, the goal being to make sure that people in the state are cared for and employed. After all, when people are off the welfare or unemployment rolls, it results in more taxes for the entire state. California alone spends $400 million running just one of these programs.

Yet the people who are getting paid to help the unemployed in California aren't even California state workers. Rather, they're residents of India and Mexico. They're cheap foreign laborers, being paid with California tax dollars to answer the telephone when unemployed Californians need help.

California is not the only state engaging in this practice of outsourcing state programs. Stella Hopkins of the *Charlotte Observer* conducted a survey that found that forty states, as well as the District of Columbia, have food stamp help desks that use operators in other countries.

Why are states staffing these employment services with cheap overseas labor when the goal is to help get their own residents back into the workforce? The logic behind this escapes me at every level. In fact, it escapes just about everyone who gives it a moment of thought. The reason is obvious. As Kerry Korpi, of the American Federation of State, County and Municipal Employees, told my show, "This was a program that's set up to help people who can't find a job. So, somebody's calling for help on food stamps and they're calling India. It's a cruel irony. If, instead, that job was located here in the United States, maybe there would be one less person who needed food stamps."

State outsourcing is doubly damaging in that the use of foreign labor distances the states from the people they are supposed to serve. It affects residents on a personal level. When someone calls, say, a food stamp help desk, how is a customer service representative located on the other side of the world going to instruct them about how to go to a particular nearby market that takes food stamps, or which subway or bus line will take them there? Outsourcing jobs that are designed for the well-being of state residents raises the depersonalization of the outsourcing process to a whole new level of irony.

Using taxpayer dollars to pay foreign workers is creating a lot of angry voters, and rightfully so. Washington State came under fire when it was revealed that not only were the phone service operators of its food stamp program based in Bangalore, but the software programming for the Washington State Health Care Authority was being coded in part in Hyderabad. Tom Fitzsimmons, the governor's chief of staff, defended the practice, stating, "We want the most value for our technology investment. And the most value adds up to perhaps including teams of vendors that include capacities from offshore." That must have been cold comfort to Washington's out-of-work software programmers.

But Washington is learning that outsourcing doesn't always live up to its promise of being quick, efficient, and cheap. The Indian subcontractor building Washington's new health authority software has repeatedly delayed delivery.

As I noted earlier, Indiana's Department of Workforce Development (DWD) signed a $15 million contract with one of India's most prominent outsourcing firms, Tata. The contract was slated to bring sixty-five Indian workers, who work at a reduced wage, to Indiana in order to develop new computer programs that would replace the state's existing tax and unemployment claims processing system. When word of the deal leaked out, citizens and legislators were incensed—in no small part because the DWD is charged with helping Indiana workers find jobs. Within a month of the deal, Indiana governor Joe Kernan had the contract canceled under a new initiative called "Opportunity Indiana."

Such moves have yet to stem the tide. Proponents of outsourcing state jobs claim that outsourcing saves the taxpayers money because they can provide the services for a reduced rate. But proponents can't quantify those savings across the board. In fact, if they had given those call center jobs to people living within the state, those people would be paying taxes back to the state. That strikes me— and, I would hope, most people—as a win-win solution for the state and its citizens. Because, as I've said, people in other countries don't pay taxes to the United States. That money goes overseas and stays there.

Who would resist giving those jobs to state workers and providing such an obvious benefit to our states? Well, one is Harry Miller, president of the Information Technology Association of America (ITAA), the leading trade association for the IT industry. Miller wants to make sure that outsourcing isn't stifled by any government attempts to keep the jobs at home. Miller told my show, "Our study showed that offshore competition added ninety thousand more jobs to the U.S. last year, will add three hundred thousand jobs to the U.S. by the year 2008. We don't need this kind of restrictionist legislation."

That may be the result of his group's study, but that's all it is—a study by a special-interest group. I don't think his logic would sway American workers who are in need of jobs and would be happy to be doing the jobs that are shipped to other countries.

Another group that doesn't like the idea of keeping those jobs here is the National Foundation for American Policy. That group, whose board includes former aides to Vice President Cheney, President Reagan, and President Bush, released a study that claims that legislation to block the shipment of American jobs to cheap foreign labor markets is unconstitutional. Stuart Anderson, the director of this organization, told me the courts have found that states don't have the right to make their own foreign policy or their own trade agreements or trade policies—that in doing so, states are contravening existing U.S. trade agreements and making their own foreign commerce decisions. He also stated that states like California could face trade retaliation. Anderson believes that "belligerent activity" like restricting outsourcing deals will only do harm to our nation.

It's hard to see what type of retaliation countries like India, Thailand, the Philippines, or Romania would inflict on California. Would they stop outsourcing their jobs over here? Since they don't outsource to us, that's not an issue. The real issue is that those countries have bid on state—not federal—contracts and have won them at the expense of American jobs. Not to mention that awarding those contracts overseas contributes to our out-of-control trade deficit.

But Anderson believes that the trade deficit is good for workers because, as he told me, "When you look at France and Germany, they have a trade surplus. And because of the inflexible labor markets they have twice the unemployment rate as the U.S. . . . The U.S. actually has a surplus in white-collar services we sell abroad. So, we have actually more to lose in retaliation."

The fact is, that surplus has decreased by 36 percent. Our deficit has increased dramatically. To my mind, it may be time to get belligerent and start leveling the playing field. Anderson, however, makes the case that the United States benefits from lower prices and that the real issue is job training and education. I don't think helping consumers save a few cents on trinkets and T-shirts is worth the loss of American jobs. And I still haven't heard from Anderson—or anyone else—about where we're going to get all those jobs that we plan on training everyone for.

To be fair, it appears that many state legislatures were not aware that portions of their food stamp and employment help desks were located in other countries. In many cases, elected officials have tried to act quickly to address the issue. More than two-thirds of our state legislatures are working on bills to limit outsourcing of state contracts. Governors in Minnesota, Michigan, Arizona, and North Carolina have bypassed their state legislators and acted on their own to block the outsourcing of state jobs. Florida state senator Walter "Skip" Campbell proposed legislation to stop the outsourcing of jobs after the state gave a $280 million contract to Convergys, which maintains call centers in India. Campbell, like many others, found it reprehensible that Florida taxpayers should have to surrender their tax dollars to keep the economy of India afloat while American states struggle with joblessness. The senator took a personal interest in the issue after his brother-in-law was laid off when his job was sent to India. Campbell's bill was eventually defeated, in part because of opposition from Governor Jeb Bush, the president's brother.

A similar bill in New Jersey met the same fate. A bill to ban outsourcing of state contracts easily passed that state's senate, with a unanimous vote of 40–0. Then it died in the assembly state government committee, where it sat for over a year without being given a hearing or a vote. Part of the reason for its demise was the Information

Technology Association of America, which opposed the bill and actively lobbied against it.

Even if such measures do become law, there will be loopholes large enough to sail a cargo ship through. While many states are trying to keep state services in America, a lot of them haven't stipulated that those jobs actually be performed by Americans. This allows for a form of insourcing that uses foreign workers, not American citizens, to perform jobs. Many of these workers come to the United States using what are known as H-1B and L-1 visas. They are still foreign nationals, and they often work at a fraction of the pay of their American coworkers. Since they aren't American citizens, they don't pay taxes here. Many of them are taught skills while here and then take their expertise and their money and return home. (This most certainly would have been the case with Indiana and its Tata contract.)

Even worse, some of this legislation doesn't take into account that while the work is being done in America, it is being done by foreign companies. They don't have to pay into the U.S. tax base, either.

What's striking about this dilemma is that so many people still don't get it and still aren't willing to accept it as reality. When Daniel Henninger of the *Wall Street Journal* wrote about my stand against outsourcing, he said, "What's weird is what a lonely fight it turns out to be." As far as Henninger was concerned, the only place where people cared about outsourcing was in a television place he called "Louville," apparently thinking that a novel and clever term for my show. He had, after all, used similar scathing wit in comparing me to Linda Blair, Dennis Kucinich, and Paul of Tarsus.

But like so many analysts, journalists, and politicians who aren't willing to face the facts, Henninger overlooked the fact that outsourcing is a very big deal to many people, not just to me. The proof is evident across the country: As of this writing, thirty-five states have legislation pending that prohibits the outsourcing of state jobs to overseas workforces. Pennsylvania has even gone as far as to create legislation that would require companies that outsource more than a hundred jobs to a foreign country to disclose that fact. If those companies are outsourcing that many jobs, they would not be eligible to receive state aid or state or local contracts for seven years. The California state senate overwhelmingly approved a bill that would require state contractors to certify that contract work would be done by people living in the state of California. It also approved a second bill that would require employers to state the numbers of workers employed in California, other states, and overseas as part of their payroll reports.

But the only state to successfully get anti-outsourcing written into law is Tennessee. In May, Governor Phil

Bredesen signed a bill that made Tennessee the first state to give businesses incentives to keep their jobs in the state and not send them overseas. State procurement officials involved in call center and data processing bids are to give preference to contractors who agree to use only U.S. workers. The bill had, as you might expect, received strong support from the state's legislators.

Why is Tennessee the only state to have succeeded thus far? Because lobbying pressure has kept other states from passing such laws. They are not interested in what voters want, only in what their corporate members want. And since lobbying groups don't represent people like you and me, the interests of the vast number of citizens get shoved to the side. Lobbyists are committed to the interests of the corporations that pay them, and that's the sum total of their focus.

Lobbying firms and corporations may not care about individual citizens, but that doesn't mean they are unaware of us or completely impervious to our criticisms. They watch the news, they read papers, and they are aware that Americans are not happy about the jobs that are being sent overseas. To defuse the outsourcing backlash, or sidestep it altogether, a number of companies have created internal guidelines or written memos on how to address the subject. These are designed to be used by human resources personnel and management as a way to sanitize the issue for employee consumption. Essentially, such documents are meant to tout the benefits of outsourcing for the whole company, while reassuring those remaining employees (who have not been outsourced) that their jobs are secure and that the company is committed to them for the long term. Which, as you and I know, lasts only until the next time the company decides cheap labor will improve its balance sheet.

These documents and memos are insidious, they are deceptive, and they do nothing to create an honest dialogue with anyone involved in the process. Employees are lied to, management cowers behind PR-produced spin, and everyone fears the motives of everyone else. The employees worry that management will ax them at the drop of a hat, while management fears that employees may quit over their treatment or, worse, sabotage operations if they feel they are being exploited. The lack of openness in dealing with the issue creates a culture of fear that runs from top to bottom of the company.

My opinions on this subject appear to have heightened the fear in the executive suite. While I believe I'm extremely up-front and straightforward with guests on *Lou Dobbs Tonight,* there are proponents of outsourcing who feel as if a call to join me on my show is akin to an ambush. Those who feel this way have recently been provided with a "cheat sheet" on how to handle an invitation from me, courtesy of the magazine *Securities Industry News*. It's so entertaining—and transparent—as an example of the double-talk being employed by companies, that I thought I'd share it with you here:

What to Say When Lou Dobbs Calls

MAY 31, 2004
SECURITIES INDUSTRY NEWS
COPYRIGHT © 2004 THOMSON MEDIA INC.
ALL RIGHTS RESERVED.

With jobs still scarce, and a presidential election in November, the outsourcing phenomenon has emerged as a kind of political third rail, with a powerful backlash uniting to oppose it. One of the most outspoken critics of offshore outsourcing is Lou Dobbs, the television newsman and host of CNN's Lou Dobbs Tonight. *In addition to offering up a steady barrage of criticism on his show, Dobbs maintains a Web site listing U.S. companies that are "exporting America" by sending jobs overseas, and/or employing low-cost foreign labor instead of American workers.*

Securities Industry News *correspondent Carol E. Curtis asked William Bierce, an outsourcing attorney with Bierce and Kenerson in New York City, for some thoughts about what to say if you get caught on the media hot seat by a journalist like Dobbs, and are asked to defend the practice of outsourcing.*

Securities Industry News: *How do you respond to charges that outsourcing is costing America jobs?*

William Bierce: You say that I will be responsible, but also efficient and effective. Outsourcing is business process management. It's not just about jobs; it is about making my business enterprise competitive.

Securities Industry News: *Who else is in your corner?*

Bierce: Some Democratic politicians, including Senator Joseph Lieberman [D-Conn.], have recently made the point that in their view, offshore outsourcing is not a root cause of America's lack of competitiveness. Rather, they say it is due to our educational system, and our system of entitlements. Our goal is to maintain the competitiveness of our global enterprises. If your enterprise is inefficient, you will wind up outsourcing or getting restructured. So the alternative to the exporting of jobs is to squeeze out inefficiency.

Securities Industry News: *What do you say to critics who call outsourcing unpatriotic?*

Bierce: To these doubters, I would reply that, "if you want to make it unpatriotic, you should enact a law." Significantly, despite the political hue and cry over outsourcing, there is no bill that would seriously threaten this trend. You are moving jobs around. The process whereby business value is added has been changed forever by the digital revolution.

Securities Industry News: *Can you recommend a short answer?*

Bierce: Your sound bite should be, "Lou, we are not doing outsourcing. We are redesigning our organization so that we can be competitive in the digital age, which requires us to identify where best to find resources, and where to deliver them."

How's that for an insight into the workings of Corporate America? It's no wonder Americans don't trust big companies and their executives. When these people are not defrauding their investors or defending their pay packages, they're trying to hide their motives.

Try as they might, lobbyists and their client corporations cannot change the public's widely held view that outsourcing isn't good for our country over the long term. The thousands of e-mails that I've received are only one indication of that. The fact that legislators are getting pressure from their voters is a more important indication. People who are fed up band together and become their own pressure groups, and politicians have to sit up and take notice. While not possessing the same levels of funding that lobbyists can bring to bear, citizens groups can attract enough media attention to make local politicians squirm in their seats.

That's exactly what happened over the past year as state outsourcing became headline news. Politicians were taken to task for putting the economic and labor needs of their constituencies dead last. Some of the elected officials initially responded in ways that sounded as though they had their own cheat sheets. By and large, they eventually had to drop their defenses and address the fiscal downside of the issue. A few politicians, to their credit, stood up right from the start and said that outsourcing state jobs was just plain wrong.

The groundswell of concern on the part of legislators is a relatively recent phenomenon. The concern is certainly heightened by the fact that we're in an election year and a lot of people still don't have jobs. Nonetheless, the issue is on the table, and Tennessee's recent ruling on outsourcing proves that pro-outsourcing lobbyists can't claim total victory—yet.

For the states, there's a long way to go before they resolve the inherent problems that outsourcing creates. As states deal with the aftermath of the recession and look for ways to correct their own budget deficits, they're putting bigger burdens on their taxpayers. By relying on individual taxpayers and not corporate taxes to make up the shortfall, our government is already squeezing its citizens. Nearly two-thirds of corporations don't pay federal taxes, and many of them enjoy big breaks at the local level.

Outsourcing may seem like a cheap solution to fiscal shortfalls in the near term, but the long-term ramifications are sure to be destructive. Paying millions—or hundreds of millions—of dollars to insourced foreign nationals or to overseas laborers ensures that what little money the states do have is on a one-way trip out of the country. How can the states hope to recoup lost tax revenue when they aren't making a concerted effort to employ the workers who are on their own unemployment lines?

The solution is a simple equation. If you put a resident of the state to work, that person pays taxes. They are taken off the unemployment rolls and thus do not need state assistance. Employment also increases their purchasing power, adding to the state coffers through sales taxes. The money moves within the state, benefiting everybody in the state.

The inability of state legislatures to prevent this kind of abuse of state workers and taxpayers is one of the most glaring examples yet of the control that companies and special interests have over our political agenda. You'd be hard-pressed to find an American worker who agrees with the practice, yet their needs—and their votes—have become subservient to the demands of Corporate America. Look no further than the failed New Jersey proposal, which passed without a single dissenting vote yet was doomed to failure through the efforts of a group that supports outsourcing because it improves the bottom line of its member companies.

We're a country, first and foremost, of men, women, and children who should expect that our government is behaving in our interests at every level, whether it be national, state, county, or town. When people aren't working and are actively being harmed by our government's policies, then it's obvious that citizens are not the top priority of our elected officials. Like a bad investment, we've given our votes to people who are more concerned with those organizations and companies that stuff their pockets come election time. Our votes as individuals aren't considered, nor are they even required. Corporations are making the decisions for our lawmakers, and we've become incidental.

Until this state of affairs is straightened out, we'll continue to lose jobs to other countries, and our tax base will erode. And when our government wonders why its citizens can no longer carry the tax burden after their jobs are gone, all it will have to do is look at whose interests it has really been serving all these years.

NINE

A Simple Choice

Any government, like any family, can for a year spend a little more than it earns. But you and I know a continuation of that habit means the poorhouse.

—FRANKLIN DELANO ROOSEVELT

The United States has become the largest debtor nation on the face of the earth, the largest debtor nation in the history of the world. Our national debt combined with our trade debt has reached almost the same level as our yearly gross domestic product. Our combined federal budget deficits and trade deficits are approaching 10 percent of GDP. We are writing mountains of IOUs to foreign countries to pay for our excessive spending, both as a government and as consumers. Those IOUs to foreigners are claims on our assets, and they will come due. And although many economists say our debt is not a problem in the long run, I believe the due date will arrive sooner than most of us imagine.

How can the world's wealthiest nation, the world's only superpower, find itself in the grip of such monstrous debt? First, our national debt has risen because our government has accelerated federal spending to fight terrorism and two wars and to add expensive social programs. Second, because tax revenues have been reduced by the Bush tax cuts and, until recently, by slow economic growth. Third, our trade debt has risen because American consumers are out of control. Our household debt is at record levels, personal bankruptcies are at an all-time high, and we continue to buy, and buy voraciously. And we are buying imported goods on credit. Fourth, because we have no choice but to buy imported goods, since we don't produce enough products in this country. We're dependent on foreigners not only for our oil and gasoline but for our steel, cement, clothing, lumber, electronic appliances, computers, and a host of other products that we once made in America. And fifth, because we don't produce enough goods and services that the rest of the world wants to buy or can buy from us.

Because we don't export as much as we import, we must either curtail our international shopping or continue to buy on credit and add further to our trade debt. In the very recent past we didn't have this problem. Until 1976 we produced and exported more than we imported.

But in the decades since, we've increased our consumption—and reduced our production—at such a staggering rate that we find ourselves under a crushing level of debt. The situation is steadily getting worse, because now we're producing less for ourselves as well as for our trading partners. The first reason for our failure to compete effectively is our one-sided and badly negotiated "free" trade agreements. Other countries retain barriers to the goods and services we export, effectively preventing us from paying down that debt with goods that we produce here. Meanwhile, our consumers keep buying imports, and our deficit increases.

The second reason is directly related to outsourcing and offshoring. We're shutting down our domestic factories and sending our jobs overseas. So even if, by some unlikely stroke of national will, we made a decision to immediately stop buying from foreign countries, we couldn't. We simply don't produce enough of our own goods to meet our own demand. We've reduced manufacturing in industries such as automotive, electronics, timber, and steel to the point that our entire production capacity is too feeble to meet even our own requirements. We've handed those industries over to other countries, with full awareness that we will be dependent on them for those goods for the foreseeable future.

Our lack of self-reliance and inability to produce our own goods is seen by most economists as simply a global economy at work, but our growing dependency on the rest of the world for commodities and finished goods alike is, in my opinion, reason for considerable concern, if not alarm. Not only is the industrialization of China, much of Asia, and Eastern Europe creating rising demand for commodities and capital, it is setting the stage for serious global competition that the United States is not in a position to win. Regional trade is rising dramatically, further adding to the contest for raw products and, ultimately, finished products as well. Regional trade in Asia, among countries like India, Korea, and China, rose 47 percent last year. Asian countries and companies are intensifying their search for new and emerging markets for their goods, and they're increasingly turning to their neighbors. The United States may be importing all the goods it wants from these countries right now, but there may come a time when that won't be possible. There is absolutely no assurance that China will always maintain its currency at artificially low levels that allow us to buy their products relatively cheaply. And what happens when we have flooded the world with so many American dollars that our currency declines further, making imports even more expensive? And what would happen to our economy if countries that own immense amounts of our securities and debt decide to reduce their holdings? Our economic dependency could carry an extremely high price.

As if it wasn't bad enough that we no longer manufacture goods that are basic to our national needs, Corporate

America, with the full support of the past two administrations, has begun shipping high-paying jobs to other countries, from legal, research, engineering, and medical services to accounting, finance, operations, and software development. These are high-end professional and service jobs that the free traders told us would replace the millions of manufacturing jobs that we've lost. Not long ago, those same free traders were declaring that our exports of high-technology products would one day offset our weak performance in the export of other products. But now the high-technology trade surplus we had as recently as three years ago has turned into a $27.5 billion deficit. Even though we've been running trade deficits in goods and products, we've managed to run a trade surplus in services for years. But now we're losing that advantage as well. Our surplus in the service sector dropped to $60 billion last year, a significant and worrisome decline from 1997, when we had a $91 billion surplus. Not even the heaviest doses of faith-based free trade can alter the facts or the predicament in which we now find ourselves.

Our annual trade deficit amounts to 5 percent of our GDP. Estimates by the Economic Policy Institute suggest that 99 percent of this deficit results from spending on goods and products that we no longer manufacture in the United States. That should be alarming to even the most ardent free trade advocates. Our few attempts to redress the one-sided free trade agreements with the rest of the world have largely met with failure. The World Trade Organization's 2003 meeting in Cancun was an abject failure on all counts, and the U.S. agenda was effectively derailed. Not that we should expect much from that organization on our behalf anyway: The United States has lost more than 80 percent of the cases in which it has been the defendant before the WTO tribunals, and the WTO has ruled against the United States in more than 90 percent of the cases tried against Asian countries.

Those of us who believe that our government has failed abysmally to enforce environmental and labor standards, to create equitable and balanced trade agreements, and to call for a rational approach to our trade policies have been called protectionists by the administration. Yet neither President Bush nor anyone else in his administration has leveled this charge at countries that retain significant trade barriers. No one in the administration has called the European Union or Japan protectionist, yet they regularly maintain trade surpluses with the United States. Nor has the administration complained loudly that China doesn't buy enough American products, maintains tariffs that are barriers to U.S. exports, doesn't pay its workers a minimum wage, and fails to enforce workplace safety standards. Instead, both the Bush and Clinton administrations surrendered to the Chinese on a wide range of commercial issues including contract law, intellectual property rights, and reciprocity. And you won't hear this president or his cabinet complaining about China's labor regulations and pay, either. That wouldn't be good for business.

Labor organizations in this country have tried to do what the Bush administration won't. They've at least tried to stem the exodus of manufacturing jobs and the outsourcing of service jobs to cheap labor markets by demanding that our trading partners live up to agreed-upon trade practices that were made conditions of gaining access to our consumer market. The AFL-CIO filed a complaint with the U.S. trade office claiming that China, as a U.S. trade partner, has not lived up to the labor standards of our trade agreements. This includes enforcing the maximum number of hours a laborer is allowed to work, adhering to and enforcing safety standards, and ensuring a minimum wage. Right now China's wages are between 47 and 86 percent lower than they should be, which reduces China's production costs and keeps its exports cheaper than they should be. China's indifference to labor standards means there is no way that American labor will ever be able to compete with Chinese labor.

The AFL-CIO claimed that the Chinese had cheated on our agreements, and invoked the Trade Act of 1974 and asked the U.S. trade representative to put things right. Specifically, they asked for three things: (1) that the United States impose trade remedies against China that are equal to the amount of revenue gained from the cheating, (2) that the United States fashion an agreement that says our country will reduce these remedies only upon verification of China's meeting the labor benchmarks that have been ignored, and (3) that the United States not enter into any more agreements with the World Trade Organization until the WTO mandates that all its members meet United Nations International Labor Organization standards. The Bush administration would not support the AFL-CIO position. That wouldn't be good for business.

And the abundance of ridiculously cheap labor in China is its principal attraction for foreign companies that are investing hundreds of billions of dollars to build plants, factories, and infrastructure in China—and exporting jobs there by the shipload. Millions of manufacturing jobs have been effectively shipped to China and other countries, and entire industries here have been shut down. While the rise in wages of all American workers has been depressed by offshoring and outsourcing, labor union membership has been the hardest hit. In fact, the unions have been increasingly marginalized in the past two and a half decades. Their influence has diminished as their membership has suffered a dramatic decline, falling by almost half since the late '70s. Despite this precipitous drop, Corporate America is still quick to blame organized labor for its need to outsource jobs to cheap foreign labor markets. The outsourcing American multinational corporations and their consultants say that unions have driven up wages to a point where the only recourse is to move American factories and plants overseas and replace American workers with cheap foreign labor. The multinationals and their consultants also blame our burdensome legal system, high tax rates, excessive workplace regulation, and environmental laws.

Personally, I think there's no question that labor unions became too powerful in the 1960s and '70s in this country, just as I think there's no question that Corporate America is too powerful now. But everyone acknowledges that almost every benefit that working men and women in this country enjoy is directly attributable to the efforts of labor organizations and unions. I strongly believe that unless a countervailing power to that of Corporate America asserts itself, the American worker faces less opportunity and lower pay in the years ahead. Labor unions were once that countervailing power, but no longer. I've discussed this issue with the AFL-CIO's John Sweeney and Richard Trumka a number of times on the show. Trumka says, "We think it's a red herring to say that it's unions that are to blame for this. These are bad [trade] policies,

Lou. They got outnegotiated. They should have done a better job at negotiating. They should have done a better job in enforcing the laws. Together, working with management, I know something. I know the American worker can compete with anybody in the world. And that's what we want to do—just compete, beat them at their own game."

Trumka believes that filing a complaint and demanding sanctions is the only way to stem the tide of job losses this country has experienced in recent years. He also feels that President Bush and his administration have turned a deaf ear to the plight of American working men and women. "This president has no policies to go forward," says Trumka. "He has not enforced the trade laws that are on the books. We want him to do that. This is an opportunity for him to stand up and prove to the American worker that he really does support them. If he doesn't do it, then we'll know where he stands. He'll stand with the multinationals against American workers. We hope that he does the right thing. That he enforces our laws. That he insists the Chinese start to enforce their laws so that workers . . . in China and the U.S. can have a better life, and trade can start to work for everybody in the world and not just the privileged few."

The subtext here is that American workers can compete if they're willing to accept the low wages—and dismal living conditions—of cheap foreign laborers. And that is certainly the choice that has been forced upon us by Corporate America's offshoring and outsourcing of jobs: either accept lower living standards or begin to balance our trade and restrict outsourcing. Our multinationals want the best of all possible worlds: to draw upon the world's greatest capital markets and enjoy the benefits of the strongest legal, political, and economic systems ever created, while exporting jobs to cheap overseas markets and selling those goods and services into the richest consumer market in the world. And all that the multinationals are asking of us is that we give up our quality of life, our way of life, for their profitability.

As I've mentioned, *The Economist* magazine accused me of embarking "on a rabidly antitrade editorial agenda," which demonstrates that either they haven't been paying close attention to what I'm saying or they consider my concern for the living standards of working men and women and for the quality of life of America's middle class to be "antitrade." Would that mean, then, that *The Economist* is antiworker and anti-American? I know of no one, least of all myself, who is recommending that America not trade with the rest of the world. No one wants America to withdraw from the world of international commerce. And the writers of *The Economist* are intelligent enough to comprehend that we don't face an either-or proposition in conducting our trade policy, despite the Bush administration's campaign rhetoric. The choice we face is whether we will demand reciprocal benefits, mutuality, and balance in our trading relationships or will simply continue policies and practices that strip us of our wealth and destroy our way of life. That choice, in my opinion, is clear. What is not clear is whether Americans will demand that our government *make* the correct choice.

TEN

Finding the Solutions

The significant problems we face cannot be solved at the same level of thinking we were at when we created them.

—ALBERT EINSTEIN

We find ourselves confronted with a number of difficult choices in the months and years ahead, choices that will likely determine our economic future, the kind of society we will live in, and our nation's role in the world. And the choices are made more difficult by our reluctance to engage in a public dialogue dealing with the real issues and to discuss possible answers to questions that, apparently, Corporate America and Washington would prefer not even be asked.

I've tried here to lay out what I believe are some of the most critical issues, to pose the tough questions raised by the outsourcing of American jobs to cheap foreign labor markets and by the Bush administration's wholesale pursuit of free trade agreements. While outsourcing has cost hundreds of thousands of jobs, millions more are at risk.

While we pursue free trade, our status as the world's largest debtor nation worsens. Even if the result is more profits for multinational corporations, do we truly believe that exporting those jobs will lead to a better life in this country, for our workers? Even if we are buying more and cheaper goods from our trading partners, do we really believe that our quality of life is better and that we should sustain permanent dependency and indebtedness? Or will outsourcing and free trade lead to further, wider gaps between the wealthy and our middle class? Should we simply hope that Corporate America will find a social conscience and voluntarily restrain its outsourcing to a minimum? Should we continue to permit the exportation of our knowledge base, technology, and capital to other countries to provide the products and services for export back to America? Or should we rely on public policy, regulation, tariffs, and quotas to protect our standard of living? Or should we share the blind faith of many in Corporate America and Washington, in the power of a free market to resolve these questions?

Federal Reserve chairman Alan Greenspan is a keeper of that faith. Earlier this year, talking about the relationship between anemic job creation and the outsourcing of American jobs, Greenspan said, "In response to these strains and the dislocations they cause, a new round of protectionist steps is being proposed. These alleged cures would make matters worse rather than better. They would do little to create jobs; and if foreigners were to retaliate, we would surely lose jobs. Besides enhancing education, we need to further open markets here and abroad to allow our workers to compete effectively in the global marketplace."

Education is certainly a critical component of any long-term strategy to improve our competitiveness, but it's an impossibility as a short-term strategy, and the threat of outsourcing American workers is immediate. But for what jobs and careers would the Fed chairman have us "enhance education"? It is not as if outsourcing is only affecting uneducated Americans—quite the contrary. The unemployment statistics for workers in the computer science industries, for instance, are nothing short of shocking. The unemployment rate for computer hardware engineers in the United States is a staggering 9 percent.

We shouldn't be overly surprised that our leaders and institutions have produced very few answers to the most important questions we face today. Our collective reflex has been either to ignore the challenges of the world as it is or to assume, whether out of ideology, political faith, or sheer apathy, that the world we want will one day arrive. And while we don't have as much information and evidence as we would like, that will always be the case. Lack of information isn't a sufficient reason to ignore the evidence we do have about the impact of our free trade policies and outsourcing, or to avoid considering whether we could better serve our national economic, social, and political interests; nor is it sufficient reason to further defer our judgment on the kind of society and nation that will result from continuing current policies versus setting a new path. I have no doubt whatsoever that the United States must pursue a new direction in our trade policies, seek balance in our international trade, and end the wholesale export of American jobs. Our political leaders will set that direction, and the choices that voters make this year are more important than ever in determining whether we will succeed in setting a new course before it's too late.

It is now clear that most Republicans will support free trade at any cost and not temper their commitment to the WTO, NAFTA, CAFTA, or FTAA, that the Bush administration will continue to drive free trade agreements that will only worsen our trade deficit, and that most Republicans will in no way lessen their endorsement of the outsourcing practices of U.S. multinationals. It is also clear that Corporate America will not end the outsourcing of American jobs to cheap foreign labor markets without government intervention. That intervention is unlikely as long as the alliance between big business and both major political parties remains intact, and it's stronger now than ever before because the Democrats have surrendered their historical support of workers. There is simply no opposing political force to that alliance so long as the Democrats remain in it. But there are some signs that more than a few Democrats want to return to their core social values and are tiring of their junior-partner status in the alliance.

It is not at all clear what the Democrats will do. The New Democrat Clinton administration brought us NAFTA and the WTO. The Democratic party for the past decade and a half has all but abandoned its commitment to working men and women and embraced the New Democrat philosophy. Senator Kerry has supported free trade, but also has tried to move closer to his party's traditional position on labor. The senator's lambasting of "Benedict Arnold CEOs" who outsource American jobs put him at the forefront of those supporting workers. Now Kerry and the Democrats face a critical political decision on the issue of outsourcing and free trade. They are hardly differentiated from President Bush and the Republicans on Iraq and the Middle East, and even Senator Kerry's calls for a restoration of international alliances and multilateralism are only a mild departure from the status quo. A strong position on the importance of balanced trade, on reducing our national dependency not only on oil but on nearly all imports, and on preserving the quality of life for American workers would be differentiating, but such a position carries great electoral risks as well. Can the Democrats successfully talk about the importance of reducing our trade deficits and achieving balanced trade without being tarred by the Bush administration as protectionists? Can Senator Kerry call for strengthening our manufacturing base and reducing our import dependency without having Republicans successfully label him a nativist? Will Democrats be able to demand the end of outsourcing American jobs to third world cheap labor markets and still avoid being called antibusiness and "economic isolationists"? And even if they are successful in taking a principled stand on these issues and overcoming the campaign attacks, which will surely be vigorous, will voters respond? Are working men and women ready to support a party that will act in their interests, and show up at the polls in November in sufficient numbers to vote for a candidate who takes such a position? I sure don't know the answers to those political strategy questions, but I do know that unless the Republicans moderate their free trade and outsourcing positions, or the Democrats take a pro-worker position, we will be well on our way to losing our middle class.

Senator Kerry's call for tax credits for U.S. multinationals to hire Americans, and tax incentives for those companies to bring their profits back to this country, are good first steps. But solving the problems of outsourcing and massive trade deficits will require a broad change in our trade policy: the creation of a comprehensive trade strategy that will narrow and then eliminate our trade deficits and end the outsourcing of our jobs.

And strategy, not blind faith, is required. The conventional wisdom of Corporate America and Washington held that there was no reason to worry about millions of American manufacturing jobs lost to cheap overseas markets, because the United States was in transition from a manufacturing economy to a service economy. Growth in our service sector would be so strong that these manufacturing jobs would be replaced by high-value service jobs. But not only has that not happened, our trade surplus in services is actually falling, down by 35 percent since 1997.

The first requirement of any short-term solution is to see the world as it is, not as Corporate America and Washington tell us it is. They haven't been right yet. Our jobs continue to be outsourced; our trade deficit continues to worsen.

I believe that Congress must now act. Corporate America will not end outsourcing on its own: It is driven to cut costs and boost short-term profits, and it will continue to claim that even if it ends the practice of outsourcing, its competitors will continue to outsource. They're probably right about that. So let's level the playing field. Congress and all state governments should immediately prohibit the outsourcing of government contracts and American jobs to cheap foreign labor. Some state legislators have introduced bills requiring that work on state government contracts be performed by Americans, but what is needed most is action at the federal level. While it may be more difficult to regulate the offshore outsourcing activities of multinational corporations, our own government should not be spending Americans' tax dollars to send government work abroad.

Our costly "free trade" agreements should be reviewed by Congress, and action taken to ensure that they are either amended to assure balanced trade or ended. As Senator Byron Dorgan (Democrat, North Dakota) put it, "Fifteen years after our beef agreement with Japan, [there is still] a 50 percent tariff on every pound of beef going into Japan. Two years after we did a bilateral trade agreement with China, they have a very large surplus with us. Our negotiators allowed them to have a 25 percent tariff on U.S. cars being shipped into China, and only a 2.5 percent tariff on any Chinese cars that would be shipped here." Our trade deficit with Japan totaled $66 billion last year; our deficit with China, $124 billion. In our pursuit of free trade at all costs, we have given away much more than we have gained. U.S. companies can easily send both their manufacturing and service jobs offshore and then reimport their own products and services with nearly unrestricted access to the U.S. marketplace. That exploitation of our trade policies must end. There is simply no way the American worker can compete with third world labor.

We must also reexamine our relationship with the World Trade Organization. Ohio Democratic congressman Dennis Kucinich, independent presidential candidate Ralph Nader, and others have called for our withdrawal from the WTO completely. This may be an extreme position, but the status quo is untenable. Kucinich also believes that the United States should require all of our trading partners to meet specific human rights and labor standards. We should be seeking to raise the standard of living globally, not reducing American standards to those of a third world country.

And we should insist that any U.S. multinational that outsources jobs should meet the same privacy standards for its American customers as if its operations were based here. Unfortunately, current federal privacy laws do not protect individuals when foreign companies misuse their personal information. This is something that absolutely must change. Several lawmakers, including U.S. senators Dianne Feinstein (Democrat, California) and Hillary Clinton (Democrat, New York), are pushing legislation to protect American consumers against such abuses. Congress must pass federal legislation to better safeguard information sent overseas. Doing so will be another important step in dissuading U.S. multinationals from sending American information and jobs abroad.

Several opponents of outsourcing, including Senator John Kerry, have proposed "right to know" legislation for call center employees. Such rules would require that workers in other parts of the world identify where they are when speaking with American customers. It would also allow consumers to make their own determination about whether they want to share private information with workers on the other side of the globe. It's unlikely this legislation will have a significant effect, but it could slow outsourcing at least marginally. A recent survey conducted by Diamond Cluster International found that more than 60 percent of IT executives are afraid of the negative publicity associated with outsourcing.

We must provide more of an incentive to keep jobs here at home. John Kerry has also proposed, in addition to several other measures, tax incentives for companies keeping American jobs at home. As part of the plan, companies creating more jobs than their previous twelve-month average would receive a refund of the payroll taxes of the new employees for two years.

Several state governors are pressing both the Bush administration and lawmakers on Capitol Hill to take similar action. Pennsylvania governor Ed Rendell told me, "We want Congress to enact the Crane-Rangel-Manzullo bill that gives tax breaks to American manufacturers who manufacture here. The administration should get behind it immediately."

The Bush administration hasn't, of course. They not only want to boost the tide of American jobs moving overseas; they also support the unrestricted flow of foreign workers that corporations are hiring in this country. The government should be working to monitor the use of H-1B and L-1 visas by companies that have been charged with using them to hire foreign labor at lower wages than their American counterparts. Not only should the use of these visas be carefully monitored, but considerable research should be done to assess both their impact on our labor market, and the value to the businesses who hire these visa holders.

Reversing decades of free-trade-at-any-cost policies, destructive free trade agreements, and chronic trade deficits will require first an honest public debate and then tough political choices. But our mistakes are reversible. We still have our destiny in our hands. Free traders believe that we can't alter the policies that led to this dangerous juncture, that only a free market can resolve the problems facing us. Their views that this country should simply accept market forces and that we don't require a trade strat-egy are to me nothing less than fatalism—an excuse not to take responsibility for our economic future. Determinism and determination have driven our nation's achievements and success for two centuries. Let's hope the same will be said of this century.

APPENDIX A

———

The Letters

Many viewers of *Lou Dobbs Tonight* have written in to share their stories of grief, pain, and protest at losing their jobs to cheap foreign workers. This is a sample of the tens of thousands of e-mails we've received. After you've read them, you will no longer think of outsourcing as a merely statistical or economic issue.

Candace Crane
Pollock Pines, California

Lou,
When I booted up this morning and saw the job numbers, my heart fell. That might sound like an odd response from someone who was unemployed for twelve months and is

now underemployed, at minimum wage half-time, but I know you won't see it as odd at all.

Now the administration, and most of the media for that matter, will be singing that happy times are instantly here again.

Not so for the millions of us that have lost work and have been financially destroyed by Bush's handling of the jobless recovery period.

As I'm sure you know, it will be a long road back for us, IF and WHEN we find good jobs, which won't be as instantly as the numbers come out. Experts say it takes one year for every month of unemployment to recover. Many of us older workers, who have a difficult time finding jobs because of ageism, will never recover.

I myself stand on the verge of filing chapter 13, and already have a lawyer on tap. He said to write to my two credit card companies first and try to get a payment holiday for six months. If they don't go for it, we'll be filing.

In your story planning, please don't forget those of us who are still suffering big-time. The outlook changes instantly on TV, but not in real life.

Thanks for all the good you do in general; I love it when you beat up on the creeps. :-)

Gordon Price
Lebanon, Pennsylvania

Thank you for defending the American worker. There are those of us who have already lost our jobs and are in re-training programs that are full of flaws. Many of us will fail because of broken promises from the government. We have lost almost everything we have. We desperately want to go back to work, but there is nowhere to go. After working over forty years, I really don't know what else to do.

Since a lot of government people are for outsourcing jobs overseas, why are they against our senior citizens outsourcing their prescriptions to Canada? Is it because large American drug companies lose money?

And I've heard that outsourcing is good because we get $89 DVD players. What if no one is working to buy those DVD players?

Sharon Zardo
Beebe, Arkansas

Thank you for speaking for those of us who can't get anyone to listen to us about jobs leaving America. My husband has lost two jobs in the last three years because of plant closings. One sold out to a competitor, because they couldn't compete with cheaper products from overseas, the other one filed bankruptcy.

He is fifty-six years old, and it is hard to find work that pays enough to pay bills. Also companies have probation periods now, so they can work you up to the end of the probation period and let you go for any reason they choose.

My husband finally found another job but it pays $6 less per hour. He has to drive farther than before, and the insurance does not take effect for three months, if they decide to keep him on. He has acid reflux, and the medicine for it costs $89.00 for 21 tablets. It's becoming more evident that the people in our government and the ones who run the companies don't care about anyone but themselves. I don't trust any politician or CEO.

Again, thanks for speaking up for America.

Mildred Maines
Randolph, Massachusetts

Dear Lou Dobbs,
You are my hero. Please continue the pressure on outsourcing USA jobs.

I am fifty-seven years old and unemployed since November 2002. I am an ex-banker with thirty-eight years in that field. My bank outsourced many jobs overseas. I have not been able to find even a temp job since the market is so bad. Every time I hear about the low unemployment rate I could scream, because I am not counted since my benefits ran out in October 2003. My best friend (a banker at another bank) will lose her job in June. She has to train her Indian replacement, and a few in her dept. must go to India to train their replacements in order to get their severance pay. What is this country coming to?

Sharon George
San Diego, California

Lou,
My husband lost his job yesterday. You guessed it: outsourcing, that wonderful policy that's SO GOOD for Americans. We live in San Diego, where rents on a two-bedroom box are easily $1,200.00 a month and wages are low.

I honestly don't know how people are piecing it together anymore.

CEOs must be having a tough time of it too. Aside from strategies to avoid jail time, they now have to worry about leaving just enough Americans with jobs so that Wal-Mart doesn't belly up.

Rick Wiese
Chesapeake, VA

Dear Mr. Dobbs,
Thank you for your efforts in shedding light on the plight of the growing number of Americans victimized by "outsourcing." I want to bring one such story to your attention. Here in southeastern Virginia, 160 mentally or physically handicapped people and 42 support staff who work with them will lose their jobs this summer because corporate America has discovered that the packages of plastic cutlery and salt packets used by the fast food and airline industries can be assembled more cheaply in China and other low-wage countries. It seems there is no shame left in America's boardrooms.

———

The List

Here is a list of companies we have confirmed are "Exporting America" as of this writing. These are U.S. companies either sending American jobs overseas or choosing to employ cheap overseas labor instead of American workers.

—LOU DOBBS, JUNE 30, 2004

3Com
3M

A
Aalfs Manufacturing
Aavid Thermal Technologies
ABC-NACO
Accenture
Access Electronics
Accuride Corporation

Accuride International
Adaptec
ADC
Adobe Air
Adobe Systems
Advanced Energy Industries
Aei Acquisitions
Aetna
Affiliated Computer Services
AFS Technologies
A.G. Edwards
Agere Systems
Agilent Technologies
AIG
Alamo Rent A Car
Albany International Corp.
Albertson's
Alcoa
Alcoa Fujikura
Allen Systems Group
Alliance Fiber Optic Products, Inc.
Alliance Semiconductor
Allstate
Alpha Thought Global
Altria Group
Amazon.com
AMD
Americ Disc
American Dawn
American Express

American Greetings
American Household
American Management Systems
American Standard
American Tool
American Uniform Company
AMETEK
AMI DODUCO
Amloid Corporation
Amphenol Corp.
Analog Devices
Anchor Glass Container
ANDA Networks
Anderson Electrical Products
Andrew Corporation
Angelica Corporation
Anheuser-Busch
Ansell Health Care
Ansell Protective Products
Anvil Knitwear
AOL
A.O. Smith
Apparel Ventures, Inc.
Apple
Applied Materials
Arkansas General Industries
Ark-Les Corporation
Arlee Home Fashions
Artex International
Art Leather Manufacturing

ArvinMeritor
Asco Power Technologies
Ashland
AstenJohnson
Asyst Technologies
AT&T
AT&T Wireless
Atchison Products, Inc.
A.T. Cross
A.T. Kearney
Augusta Sportswear
Authentic Fitness Corporation
Automatic Data Processing
Avanade
Avanex
Avaya
Avery Dennison
Axiohm Transaction Solutions
Azima Healthcare Services

B
Ball Corporation
Bank of America
Bank of New York
Bank One
Bard Access Systems
Barnes Group
Barth & Dreyfuss of California
Bassett Furniture
Bassler Electric Company

BBi Enterprises L.P.
Beacon Blankets
BearingPoint
Bear Stearns
BEA Systems
Bechtel
Becton Dickinson
BellSouth
Bentley Systems
Berdon LLP
Berne Apparel
Bernhardt Furniture
Besler Electric Company
Best Buy
Bestt Liebco Corporation
Beverly Enterprises
Birdair, Inc.
BISSELL
Black & Decker
Blauer Manufacturing
Blue Cast Denim
BMC Software
Bobs Candies
Boeing
Borden Chemical
Bose Corporation
Bourns
Bowater
Braden Manufacturing
Brady Corporation

Briggs Industries
Bristol-Myers Squibb
Bristol Tank & Welding Co.
Brocade
Brooks Automation
Brown Wooten Mills Inc.
Buck Forkardt, Inc.
Bumble Bee
Burle Industries
Burlington House Home Fashions
Burlington Northern and Santa Fe Railway

C
C&D Technologies
Cadence Design Systems
Cains Pickles
Camfil Farr
Candle Corporation
Capital Mercury Apparel
Capital One
Cardinal Brands
Carrier
Carter's
Caterpillar
C-COR.net
Cellpoint Systems
Cendant
Centis, Inc.
Cerner Corporation
Charles Schwab

The Cherry Corporation
ChevronTexaco
CIBER
Ciena
Cigna
Circuit City, Inc.
Cirrus Logic
Cisco Systems
Citigroup
Clear Pine Mouldings
Clorox
CNA
Coastcast Corp.
Coca-Cola
Cognizant Technology Solutions
Collins & Aikman
Collis, Inc.
Columbia House
Columbia Showcase & Cabinet Company
Columbus McKinnon
Comcast Holdings
Comdial Corporation
CompuServe
Computer Associates
Computer Horizons
Computer Sciences Corporation
Concise Fabricators
Conectl Corporation
Conseco
Consolidated Metro

Consolidated Ventura
Continental Airlines
Convergys
Cooper Crouse-Hinds
Cooper Industries
Cooper Tire & Rubber
Cooper Tools
Cooper Wiring Devices
Copperweld
Cordis Corporation
Corning
Corning Cable Systems
Corning Frequency Control
Countrywide Financial
COVAD Communications
Covansys
Creo Americas
Cross Creek Apparel
Crouzet Corporation
Crown Holdings
CSX
Cummins
Cutler-Hammer
Cypress Semiconductor

D
Dana Corporation
Daniel Woodhead
Davis Wire Corp.
Daws Manufacturing

Dayton Superior
DeCrane Aircraft
Delco Remy
Dell Computer
DeLong Sportswear
Delphi
Delta Air Lines
Delta Apparel
DIRECTV
Discover
DJ Orthopedics
Document Sciences Corporation
Dometic Corp.
Donaldson Company
Douglas Furniture of California
Dow Chemical
Dresser
Dun & Bradstreet
DuPont

E
Earthlink
Eastman Kodak
Eaton Corporation
Edco, Inc.
Editorial America
Edscha
eFunds
Ehlert Tool Company
Elbeco Inc.

Electroglas
Electronic Data Systems
Electronics for Imaging
Electro Technology
Eli Lilly
Elmer's Products
E-Loan
EMC
Emerson Electric
Emerson Power Transmission
Emglo Products
Engel Machinery
En Pointe Technologies
Equifax
Ernst & Young
Essilor of America
Ethan Allen
Evenflo
Evergreen Wholesale Florist
Evolving Systems
Evy of California
Expedia
Extrasport
ExxonMobil

F
Fairfield Manufacturing
Fair Isaac
Fansteel Inc.

Farley's & Sathers Candy Co.
Fasco Industries
Fawn Industries
Fayette Cotton Mill
FCI USA
Fedders Corporation
Federal Mogul
Federated Department Stores
Fellowes
Fender Musical Instruments
Fidelity Investments
Financial Technologies International
Findlay Industries
First American Title Insurance
First Data
First Index
Fisher Hamilton
Flowserve
Fluidmaster
Fluor
FMC Corporation
Fontaine International
Ford Motor
Foster Wheeler
Franklin Mint
Franklin Templeton
Freeborders
Frito-Lay
Fruit of the Loom

G

Garan Manufacturing
Gateway
GE Capital
GE Medical Systems
Gemtron Corporation
General Binding Corporation
General Cable Corp.
General Electric
General Motors
Generation 2 Worldwide
Genesco
Georgia-Pacific
Gerber Childrenswear
Gillette
Global Power Equipment Grp.
GlobespanVirata
Goldman Sachs
Gold Toe Brands
Goodrich
Goodyear Tire & Rubber
Google
Graphic Controls
Greenpoint Mortgage
Greenwood Mills
Grote Industries
Grove U.S. LLC
Guardian Life Insurance
Guilford Mills
Gulfstream Aerospace Corp.

H

Haggar

Halliburton

Hamilton Beach/Procter Silex

Harper-Wyman Company

The Hartford Financial Services Group

Hasbro Manufacturing Services

Hawk Corporation

Hawker Power Systems, Inc.

Haworth

Headstrong

Healthaxis

Hedstrom

Hein-Werner Corp.

Helen of Troy

Helsapenn Inc.

Hershey

Hewitt Associates

Hewlett-Packard

Hoffman Enclosures, Inc.

Hoffman/New Yorker

The Holmes Group

Home Depot

The HON Company

Honeywell

HSN

Hubbell Inc.

Humana

Hunter Sadler

Hutchinson Sealing Systems, Inc.
HyperTech Solutions

I
IBM
iGate Corporation
Illinois Tool Works
IMI Cornelius
Imperial Home Decor Group
Indiana Knitwear Corp.
IndyMac Bancorp
Infogain
Ingersoll-Rand
Innodata Isogen
Innova Solutions
Insilco Technologies
Intel
InterMetro Industries
International Paper
Interroll Corporation
Intesys Technologies
Intuit
Invacare
Iris Graphics, Inc.
Isola Laminate Systems
Iteris Holdings, Inc.
ITT Educational Services
ITT Industries

J

Jabil Circuit
Jacobs Engineering
Jacuzzi
Jakel Inc.
JanSport
Jantzen Inc.
JDS Uniphase
Jockey International
John Crane
John Deere
Johns Manville
Johnson & Johnson
Johnson Controls
JPMorgan Chase
J.R. Simplot
Juniper Networks
Justin Brands

K

K2 Inc.
KANA Software
Kaiser Permanente
Kanbay
Kayby Mills of North Carolina
Keane
Kellogg
Kellwood
KEMET

KEMET Electronics
Kendall Healthcare
Kenexa
Kentucky Apparel
Kerr-McGee Chemical
KeyCorp
Key Industries
Key Safety Systems
Key Tronic Corp.
Kimberly-Clark
KLA-Tencor
Knight Textile Corp.
Kojo Worldwide Corporation
Kraft Foods
Kulicke and Soffa
Kwikset

L
LaCrosse Footwear
L.A. Darling Company
Lake Village Industries
Lamb Technicon
Lancer Partnership
Lander Company
Lands' End
Lau Industries
Lawson Software
Layne Christensen
Leach International
Lear Corporation

Leech Tool & Die Works
Lehman Brothers
Leoni Wiring Systems
Levi Strauss
Leviton Manufacturing Co.
Lexmark International
Lexstar Technologies
Liebert Corporation
Lifescan
Lillian Vernon
Linksys
Linq Industrial Fabrics, Inc.
Lionbridge Technologies
Lionel
Littelfuse
LiveBridge
LNP Engineering Plastics
Lockheed Martin
Longaberger
Louisiana-Pacific Corporation
Louisville Ladder Group LLC
Lowe's
Lucent
Lund International
Lyall Alabama

M
Madill Corporation
Magma Design Automation
Magnequench

Magnetek
Maidenform
Mallinckrodt, Inc.
The Manitowoc Company
Manugistics
Marathon Oil
Marine Accessories Corp.
Maritz
Marko Products, Inc.
Mars, Inc.
Marshall Fields
Master Lock
Materials Processing, Inc.
Mattel
Maxim Integrated Products
Maxi Switch
Maxxim Medical
Maytag
McDATA Corporation
McKinsey & Company
MeadWestvaco
Mediacopy
Medtronic
Mellon Bank
Mentor Graphics Corp.
Meridian Automotive Systems
Merit Abrasive Products
Merrill Corporation
Merrill Lynch
Metasolv

MetLife
Micro Motion, Inc.
Microsoft
Midcom Inc.
Midwest Electric Products
Milacron
Modern Plastics Technics
Modine Manufacturing
Moen
Money's Foods Us Inc.
Monona Wire Corp.
Monsanto
Morgan Stanley
Motion Control Industries
Motor Coach Industries International
Motorola
Mrs. Allison's Cookie Co.
MTD Southwest
Mulox
Munro & Company

N
Nabco
Nabisco
NACCO Industries
National City Corporation
National Electric Carbon Products
National Life
National Semiconductor
NCR Corporation

neoIT
NETGEAR
Network Associates
Newell Rubbermaid
Newell Window Furnishings
New World Pasta
New York Life Insurance Co.
Nice Ball Bearings
Nike
Nordstrom
Northrop Grumman
Northwest Airlines
Nu Gro Technologies
Nu-kote International
NutraMax Products
Nypro Alabama

O

O'Bryan Brothers Inc.
Ocwen Financial
Office Depot
Ogden Manufacturing
Oglevee, Ltd
Ohio Art
Ohmite Manufacturing Co.
Old Forge Lamp & Shade
Omniglow Corporation
ON Semiconductor
Oracle
Orbitz

OshKosh B'Gosh
Otis Elevator
Outsource Partners International
Owens-Brigam Medical Co.
Owens Corning
Owens-Illinois, Inc.
Oxford Automotive
Oxford Industries

P

Pacific Precision Metals
Pak-Mor Manufacturing
palmOne
Parallax Power Components
Paramount Apparel International
Parker Hannifin
Parsons E&C
Paxar Corporation
Pearson Digital Learning
Peavey Electronics Corporation
PeopleSoft
PepsiCo
Pericom Semiconductor
PerkinElmer
PerkinElmer Life Sciences, Inc.
Perot Systems
Pfaltzgraff
Pfizer
Phillips-Van Heusen
Photronics

Pinnacle Frames
Pinnacle West Capital Corporation
Pitney Bowes
Plaid Clothing Company
Planar Systems
Plexus
Pliant Corporation
PL Industries
Polaroid
Polymer Sealing Solutions
Portal Software
Portex, Inc.
Portola Packaging
Port Townsend Paper Corp.
Power-One
Pratt & Whitney
priceline.com
Price Pfister
Pridecraft Enterprises
Prime Tanning
Primus Telecom
Procter & Gamble
Progress Lighting
ProQuest
Providian Financial
Prudential Insurance

Q
Quadion Corporation
Quaker Oats

Quantegy
Quark
Qwest Communications

R
Radio Flyer
Radio Shack
Rainbow Technologies
Rawlings Sporting Goods
Rayovac
Raytheon Aircraft
RBX Industries
RCG Information Technology
Red Kap
Regal-Beloit Corporation
Regal Rugs
Regence Group
Respiratory Support Products
R.G. Barry Corp.
Rich Products
River Holding Corp.
Robert Manufacturing Co.
Robert Mitchell Co., Inc.
Rockwell Automation
Rockwell Collins
Rogers
Rohm & Haas
Ropak Northwest
RR Donnelley & Sons

Rugged Sportswear
Russell Corporation

S
S1 Corporation
S&B Engineers and Constructors
Sabre
Safeway
SAIC
Sallie Mae
Samsonite
Samuel-Whittar, Inc.
Sanford
Sanmina-SCI
Sapient
Sara Lee
Saturn Electronics & Engineering
SBC Communications
Schumacher Electric
Scientific Atlanta
Seal Glove Manufacturing
Seco Manufacturing Co.
SEI Investments
Sequa Corporation
Seton Company
Sheldahl Inc.
Shipping Systems, Inc.
Shugart Corp.
Siebel Systems
Sierra Atlantic

Sights Denim Systems, Inc.
Signal Transformer
Signet Armorlite, Inc.
Sikorsky
Silicon Graphics
Simula Automotive Safety
SITEL
Skyworks Solutions
SMC Networks
SML Labels
SNC Manufacturing Company
SoftBrands
Sola Optical USA
Solectron
Sonoco Products Co.
Southwire Company
Sovereign Bancorp
Spectrum Control
Spicer Driveshaft Manufacturing
Spirit Silkscreens
Springs Industries
Springs Window Fashions
Sprint
Sprint PCS
SPX Corporation
Square D
Standard Textile Co.
Stanley Furniture
Stanley Works
Stant Manufacturing

Starkist Seafood
State Farm Insurance
State Street
Steelcase
StorageTek
Store Kraft Manufacturing
StrategicPoint Investment Advisors
Strattec Security Corp.
STS Apparel Corporation
Summitville Tiles
Sun Microsystems
Sunrise Medical
Suntron
SunTrust Banks
Superior Uniform Group
Supra Telecom
Sure Fit
SurePrep
The Sutherland Group
Sweetheart Cup Co.
Swift Denim
Sykes Enterprises
Symbol Technologies
Synopsys
Synygy

T
Takata Retraint Systems
Target
Teccor Electronics
Techalloy Company, Inc.

Technotrim
Tecumseh
Tee Jays Manufacturing
Telcordia
Telect
Teleflex
TeleTech
Telex Communications
Tellabs
Tenneco Automotive
Teradyne
Texaco Exploration and Production
Texas Instruments
Textron
Thermal Industries
Therm-O-Disc, Inc.
Thermo Electron
Thomas & Betts
Thomas Saginaw Ball Screw Co.
Thomasville Furniture
Three G's Manufacturing Co.
Thrivent Financial for Lutherans
Tiffany Industries
Time Warner
The Timken Company
Tingley Rubber Corp.
Tomlinson Industries
The Toro Company
Torque-Traction Manufacturing Technology
Tower Automotive
Toys "R" Us

Trailmobile Trailer
Trans-Apparel Group
TransPro
Trans Union
Travelocity
Trek Bicycle Corporation
Trend Technologies
TriMas Corp.
Trinity Industries
Triquint Semiconductor
TriVision Partners
Tropical Sportswear
TRW Automotive
Tumbleweed Communications
Tupperware
Tyco Electronics
Tyco International

U
UCAR Carbon Company
Underwriters Laboratories
UniFirst Corporation
Union Pacific Railroad
Unison Industries
Unisys
United Airlines
UnitedHealth Group
United Online
United Plastics Group
United States Ceramic Tile
United Technologies

Universal Lighting Technologies
USAA

V
Valence Technology
Valeo Climate Control
VA Software
Velvac
Veritas
Verizon
Vertiflex Products
VF Corporation
Viasystems
Vishay Intertechnology
Visteon
VITAL Sourcing

W
Wabash Alloys, L.L.C.
Wabash Technologies
Wachovia Bank
Walgreens
Walls Industries
Warnaco
Washington Group International
Washington Mutual
Waterloo Industries
Weavexx
WebEx
Weiser Lock
WellChoice

Wellman Thermal Systems
Werner
West Corporation
West Point Stevens
Weyerhaeuser
Whirlpool
White Rodgers
Williamson-Dickie Manufacturing Company
Winpak Films
Wolverine World Wide
Woodstock Wire Works
Woodstuff Manufacturing
WorldCom
World Kitchen
Wyeth
Wyman-Gordon Forgings

X
Xerox
Xpectra Incorporated
Xpitax

Y
Yahoo!
Yarway Corporation
York International

Z
Zenith
ZettaWorks